READY TO RIOT

READY TO RIOT

Nathan Wright, Jr.

Holt, Rinehart and Winston

NEW YORK • CHICAGO • SAN FRANCISCO

309.1749
W 952

To David, Nathan III, Lydia, Barbara, Carolyn,
our gifts to the world that shall be.

Contents

READY TO RIOT

1 Introduction: A City in Rebellion

It was Thursday evening, July 13, 1967. The night before the City of Newark had been rocked by a rebellion. A black cab driver had been arrested and, according to eyewitnesses, mistreated by white policemen.

For those in the bleak streets of Newark's black communities, the precise details of the report of police mistreatment were of no major concern. Repression, abuse, and a seeming disregard for the dignity and rights of persons reflect a pervasive pattern in central city life. Thus when the report was made of a gross instance of contempt for law and order on the part of the police, the local black community gave credibility to what squared with their continuing experience. The boiling tempers, fired for weeks by apparent insolence on the part of the city administration, exploded into open retaliation. The police precinct headquarters in the predominantly black Central Ward was stoned. Other acts of property destruction occurred. It appeared that on July 12 Newark might join the growing list of cities faced with major social disorders.

1

That next evening my wife, Barbara, our seventeen-year-old daughter, Barbara, whom we call "Bunky," and I had driven from our home in nearby Orange, New Jersey, to pick up a package at my Newark office. Wednesday night's disturbance had not meant terribly much to us. Only as we were preparing to leave for home did it occur to us that we might pass through or near the area of the previous night's disturbance to see just how things were.

Bunky's interest grew as we approached the neighborhood in which her mother works. Mrs. Wright serves as a nursery school leader at the Fuld Day Care Center located in the vicinity of Belmont and Seventeenth Avenues, just a block or so removed from the fourth precinct headquarters that had been stoned the night before. The Day Care Center and the police precinct are situated on the perimeter of an eight-block area bounded on the north and west by Springfield Avenue and Bergen Street; this area was to become the heart of a so-called riot zone.

We arrived at the broad intersection of Springfield and Belmont Avenues at approximately 9:30. There were clusters of some thirty to fifty people, mostly men, on each of the corners. There were large numbers of other people gathered on doorsteps. There was an air of expectancy but not of anger.

We parked our car alongside the Fidelity Union Trust Company branch building on the southwest corner of the intersection. Before I could get out, we heard a loud thud and the ringing of broken glass. At the northwest corner of the intersection a liquor store front had been broken through.

Barbara urged that we leave. I promised we would in a moment. Barbara and Bunky locked themselves in the car and I stepped onto the sidewalk adjacent to the Fidelity Union Trust.

Almost immediately there was chaos. The liquor store was ransacked. Men ran by with bottles of liquor in their hands and under their arms. The intersection swarmed with people come suddenly out of nowhere. With a sound of thunder the large plate-glass window of the bank, just a few feet from our car, was broken.

Mrs. Wright and Bunky were in near terror. Several men standing near the bank, apparently drunk and grown more aggressive in the mounting disorder, came toward us and demanded we move the car. I said we would. The men moved on.

I got back into the car. My wife was crying. "Please take us home right away," she pleaded. There was no question about it now.

We turned the next corner and headed west along Kinney Street. My wife's terror changed to outrage at what we saw. A dry cleaning establishment had been broken into. People were trying on clothes for size. Others were leaving with armloads of clothing, apparently regardless of its kind or condition.

"Nathan, the man who owns that store is one of us," my wife exclaimed. "This is terrible. It's senseless. There is simply no excuse for people to act like this. Please, please, get us out of here. Let's go home. I can't take any more of this."

Knowing something of the outrage of people who feel driven to riot, but failing to come to terms with the feelings of my own wife, I responded with a professorial air. "Barbara, while we may not like it," I said, "their behavior is a part of a social psychosis. It must be understood first, then judged." A moment or two later, recognizing Barbara's and Bunky's feelings, I added: "This does seem senseless and outrageous. I can understand the way you feel."

As we moved north along Hunterdon Street and then west along Fourteenth Avenue, sirens were screeching. More people were moving into the streets. I asked my wife and daughter if we might stay just a little longer in the disturbed area. I wanted to see at firsthand something of what I had studied and taught as the anatomy of black urban distress.

A taxicab was just ahead of us. It had stopped at the intersection. Barbara asked me to see if the cab driver would take her and our daughter home. Bunky hailed the cab, and she and her mother went home.

I had only to circle a two-block area to round out an incredible evening. I turned left onto Fairmount Avenue and then left again onto Springfield Avenue. A police road block had been set up just ahead at the corner of Springfield Avenue and Bergen Street. Hundreds of people were now milling about.

There was the sound of broken glass as someone threw a bottle into the street. It landed several hundred yards away from the intersection. One of the three policemen manning the intersection reached into a patrol car and pulled out a rifle. He fired up into the buildings in several directions. It was exactly 10:05 P.M.

Knowing that the mere presence of uniformed white policemen would be inflammatory in Newark's black heartland, I pulled my car to the curb and approached the tall policeman who had shot the rifle. "Officer," I explained, "your orders are not to shoot except in self-defense. Your disobeying the orders of your superiors is simply provoking these people to even more anger." Looking with pity at the policeman who, still holding his rifle, towered over me, I added in a moralistic tone of sadness, "Shame, Shame, Shame!"

The officer to whom I spoke seemed dumbfounded. For a moment so did the other two. Then one of them yelled out, "Get back into your car and get out of here."

As I left Newark, the sight of broken car windows, the looting of stores and the milling crowds was given dramatic intensity by the sound of sirens and the hubbub of distracted people.

The detailed story of what happened during the next several days was largely a repetition of occurrences in a growing number of black urban areas throughout the nation. The City of Newark was clearly in the midst of racial rebellion.

Altogether some ten million dollars of property was destroyed. Reportedly twenty-three black people and two white people (a police officer and a fire captain) lost their lives. Some twelve hundred persons were arrested. The National Guard and the New Jersey State Police occupied the city. Business temporarily came to a standstill. Some business establishments near to and within the ravaged area were to remain closed forever. Feelings between the races became more clearly polarized. A four-day National Conference on Black Power, scheduled months in advance of the disturbance, was about to begin on the fourth day following the official ending of the Newark revolt. Out of the immediate fury and frustration of the moment there was a call for reasoned assessment.

In the mind of the distraught black community there was a growing sense of frustration, brutality, and repression. In June 1965 the police killed a black man named Lester Long. The initial police report indicated that a policeman was leaving his car, slipped and fell, and his pistol accidently went off, killing Mr. Long. A week later a police report indicated that when Lester Long was detained in the back of a police car he assaulted the policeman with a knife. When he tried to run away, he was shot. Eyewitnesses to the killing pointed out that Lester Long was detained ostensibly for having a headlight out and a noisy muffler. He was taken away in a patrol car and returned to the scene in forty minutes. He was reported to have been seen leaving the police car. As he ran, he was shot. No one at the scene reported any evidence of a cut or of any other form of assault upon the persons of the policemen.

In August of the same year there was the death of Bernard Rich in a jail cell. The police report alleges that Mr. Rich went berserk and killed himself by banging his head against the jail cell walls. A pathologist's report indicated severe bruises on various parts of Bernard Rich's body.

A few months later, in December 1965, a seventeen-year-old youth, Walter Mathis, was shot and killed by the police. Allegedly Walter Mathis, together with four others, mugged a white man in the vicinity of a tavern. The victim reentered the tavern and said he'd been assaulted by five black youths. Two policemen, who were reported to have been drinking in the tavern, left and found five black youths two blocks away. The police indicated that the five attacked them and that Walter Mathis was killed accidentally in the assault. Eyewitnesses stated that the policemen had the young men place their hands above their heads against a wall. Then one of the policemen allegedly shot Walter Mathis. The undertaker's photograph of the victim's body is reported to show a wound that could only have been inflicted while the victim's arm was raised above his head.

Also in December 1965, the Essex County Grand Jury issued a presentment indicating a lack of law enforcement in the area of organized crime. It was discovered that there was actual overlapping in the payrolls of the Newark Police Department and an underworld related enterprise.

In January 1966 police broke into a Muslim Temple on South Orange Avenue in Newark. It was alleged that arms had been stored illegally on the temple premises. Furniture in which no arms could be stored and records unrelated to the purpose of the search were destroyed.

Much of early 1967 in the Newark black community was focused upon a proposal by the Mayor to remove some twenty-two thousand persons from the predominantly black Central Ward to clear a one hundred fifty acre tract for a state medical-dental college.

Mayor Addonizio and many leading citizens wanted the college. Plans were pushed through quickly to clear the site. Black people in the area claimed they had not been properly consulted, that adequate plans had not been made for their relocation or for their benefitting economically from the proposed reuse of the land. For the city to purchase the land for clearance, enabling state legislation was needed to raise the city's debt limit. Democratic votes in the state legislature were not sufficient for this purpose. The most massive mobilization of black people for protest in Newark's recent history was accomplished. The result: Republican legislators joined with the Democrats and raised the limit for the city's debts.

In May 1967 City Hall sources announced that one James Callaghan, a former student at St. Aloysius High School who later received a high school equivalency certificate by studying at night, was to be named Secretary to the Board of Education. The position of Secretary to the Board of Education is most crucial to the city's schools. He is accounting officer for the budget of the schools and is chief administrator for the official work of the Board of Education. Also contending for the position of Secretary to the Board of Education was a young black certified public accountant, Wilbur Parker. Mr. Parker is the holder of both a Bachelor's and a Master's degree from Cornell, the latter degree in business administration. Newspapers editorialized in his favor. Protest meetings were held. Businessmen and religious leaders spoke their support of the black community's desire that a highly qualified man, who was also a Negro, occupy the most critical position affecting a school system that is 80 percent black.

Educators and social scientists argued that the poor learning incentives of mounting numbers of failing black pupils were an issue in the debate. The Mayor's insistence on supporting the less-qualified man was said to have reinforced the notion that, however well-qualified, black men could not succeed. The Mayor was adamant. Tensions mounted in the city to a point where riot conditions were said to exist. In late June it was announced that the present Secretary of the Board would not resign and no vacancy would exist.

On July 8 a Muslim home on the East Orange-Newark line was the subject of an incident involving the police from both Newark and East Orange. The police alleged they had responded to reports of noise coming from the Muslim home that had created a disturbance of the peace. Persons who lived nearby reported no such noise and say that police had been gathering in the neighborhood for more than an hour before forcibly entering the premises and beating some of the Muslims who had come there to practice karate.

Such had been much of the negative experience of the black inhabitants of the predominantly black City of Newark. Hundreds of affidavits of alleged police brutality and municipal government repression and discrimination have been filed with the Newark Commission on Human Rights, with the Newark Branch of the National Association for the Advancement of Colored People, the Urban League of Essex County, and the Greater Newark Congress of Racial Equality.

On July 12, 1967, when John Smith, the taxicab driver who subsequently made the cover of *Time* magazine, was arrested and allegedly beaten at the hands of the police, the benighted black community seemed ripe for conflagration. These were the perceptions of the black masses, most of whom, however resentful or antagonized they might have been, were not willing to become active participants in the four days of social disorder that followed.

Shortly after the civil disorder in Newark, the State Police were asked to make their report as to its causes. Their list included five items, several of which were noted above. These were:

1. The controversy over the location of a medical-dental school in Newark;
2. The controversy regarding the selection of a Secretary to the Board of Education;
3. The reaction to alleged police abuse at the Muslim home on the East Orange-Newark city line;
4. Increased activity of militants;
5. Alleged tension over plans to hold in Newark a National Conference on Black Power.

It is evident from the State Police report and from the chronology of race-related events arousing tension and attention that at least perceived conditions of frustration and repression in the life of the city were felt to be predisposing factors for the black rebellion.

Other conditions were also present in a parallel and possibly predisposing way. Newark's life in recent years is distinguished by an unexcelled list of firsts in urban pathology. Here is a representative sampling from among major cities in the nation.

1. The highest crime rate, 1967
2. The highest tuberculosis rate
3. The highest syphilis rate
4. The highest gonorrhea rate
5. The highest maternal mortality rate
6. The highest proportionate urban tax rate
7. The highest population density (adjusted to usable land)
8. The highest proportion of land set aside for urban renewal clearance
9. The highest daytime population turnover in the nation.

The black community in Newark is clearly disadvantaged. That repression and discrimination would not be employed against those at the bottom of the social and economic scale would be out of keeping with the normal historical experience of rising ethnic groups throughout the nation. People with power tend not to share it. Indeed, they tend to work actively to prevent any take-over of power on the part of others, even where this relates basically to the control of individual fortunes. All societies strive more for order than for orderly but needed changes. Thus it would seem immediately fallacious to deny that gross discrimination did not exist in a city that has moved from an 85 percent white urban-oriented majority in 1940 to a nearly 60 percent black, strongly rural-oriented majority in 1965. Newark has been—and is—the scene of massive urban change. Such change brings disorganization.

In the pages that follow, so-called riots will be seen to be the logical result of our failure as a nation to come to terms with the depth and breadth of change in the life of our cities. Many of our cities' problems are not being solved. No one can escape the daily frustration that comes from seeing no way out of the perplexities involved.

Using Newark as an example of advanced urban blight, we shall note that many of our urban problems simply cannot be solved on the basis of past and present patterns of action. We shall see that not only black people but also white people are being compromised in our cities.

The apparent repressive attitudes of public officials—including school systems, the police, public welfare, and the other agencies of public service—will be shown to be, in large measure, symptoms of a pervasive flight from hard realities that have promised no better way of escape. What black people see as a continuing pattern of repression on the part of their fellow city-dwellers who are white is but the low-keyed counterpart of what white people see as a militant extremism allegedly predisposed to physical violence. Seen as a society boxed into frustration, the city as a whole may be said to have an ill-tempered tendency toward repression on the one hand and aggression on the other.

A quarter of a century ago Robert L. Sutherland shed some light upon the attitudes of people caught in situations of apparent impossibility. His ideas may be of tremendous significance to us today as we examine the roots of and reactions to the mounting social disorders in our cities. In his book, *Color, Class and Personality,* published in 1942, he explained that people react to frustration largely according to class-conditioned forms of behavior. His illustrations were largely from his observations of black people's reactions to white repression(In concluding our brief look at urban distress we shall reflect upon Sutherland's insights to see where they may give meaning to the behavior or reaction patterns of both black and white urbanites and suburbanites.)

While facts and figures relating to the City of Newark will be used throughout these pages, Newark must be seen as an example of what the central cities of the nation are fast becoming. Therefore it is constructive for us to look at Newark to gain an early glimpse of our possible urban future. If we do not see far more clearly what is happening—and if we do not see ourselves as possessing self-defeating and culturally induced biases that must be altered or compensated for in every urban-situated enterprise—we shall have no alternative to the fruitless charges and countercharges, the demonstrations, the effective but covert reprisals and ultimately open warfare.

It is easy to say that the mayors, the police, the educators, the welfare officials, and the other agents of the establishment in our

cities often tend to be mean, myopic, and vicious. But this is by
no means either an adequate or a strategic answer. It is also easy
to say that black militancy may trigger destruction and anarchy.
But that is not fundamentally enlightening either. All behavior
must be looked at in the civic or social context in which it occurs.
It is this context of a dysfunctional array of urban institutions
and relationships—all of which have a built-in racist bias in our
nation—that must be understood if we are to find a way out of
our mounting urban blight, distress, and peril.

These pages are a modest attempt in this direction, a direction
that is vital for the peace and preservation of the nation as a
whole. Our emphasis in examining urban distress is logically upon
its most acute manifestations in the life of our black minority. It
is that community that bears the greatest proportion of the pervasive pain imperilling the health and sanity of both our cities and
our country. Our lives are interrelated.

So to react to what is seen as black violence with counterviolence
or further repression weakens the nation. It worsens the plight of us
all. Abraham Lincoln, in a speech delivered in Edwardsville,
Illinois, in 1858, spoke these words, which are applicable to us
as we view the present fractured and bewildering conditions of
our cities:

> When you have succeeded in dehumanizing the Negro; when you
> have put him down and made it impossible for him to be but as the
> beasts of the field; when you have extinguished his soul in this world
> and placed him where the ray of hope is blown out as in the darkness
> of the damned, are you quite sure the demon you have aroused will
> not turn and rend you?
> Our reliance is in the love of liberty which God has planted in us.
> Our defense is in the preservation of the spirit which prizes liberty
> as the heritage of all men, in all lands everywhere. Destroy this spirit
> and you have planted the seeds of despotism at your own doors.
> Familiarize yourself with the chains of bondage, and you are preparing
> your own limbs to wear them. Accustomed to trample on the rights
> of others, you have lost the genius of your own independence, and
> become the fit subjects of the first cunning tyrant who rises among you.

If we are not to lose the genius of our own independence, we
must see to it that it is shared by all.

2 Dislocation and Distress

Our present so-called riots—or what some prefer to speak of as social rebellions—may be seen to have begun, at least in a low-keyed way, several decades or more ago.

Civic rebellions are a form of social insanity or psychosis. They are basically the crazed behavior of men who sense that they are driven to distraction. They represent, in a broad form, a frustrated response—in terms of both repression and aggression—to seemingly impossible circumstances that have been increasing in our cities.

In this sense civic rebellions themselves are not new. They have occurred throughout history when the pressure of unsolved problems has seemed too great for men to bear. In his *Utopia*, St. Thomas More wrote of the social, political, and economic basis for rioting during the reign of Henry VIII. Aristotle wrote in the same vein of social rebellions in his own day.[1]

As I have said, our present urban distress is associated with the

[1] See, for example, St. Thomas More's *Utopia*, edited by Edward Surtz, S.J. (New Haven, Conn.: Yale University Press, 1964).

fact that cities throughout the nation have been faced with mounting social, political, civic, and economic problems to which adequate or reasonable answers have not yet been applied. Nor have our urban problems in some crucial respects been properly defined or listened to. The fury born of frustration or the readiness to riot is structured into the present patterns of urban change and adjustment.

THE COMPOUNDING OF PROBLEMS

We may see presently how the specific kind of accelerated population change our cities have experienced since World War II has in itself been fraught with peril. John T. Cunningham, the distinguished New Jersey historian, wrote in the three hundredth-anniversary volume entitled *Newark*: "Every American city faced sweeping changes when World War II ended, but few could see in 1946 how radical the changes would be. Great areas of blight would stab at the public conscience, civil rights leaders would demand redress of century-old wrongs and industry would join residents in a flight to the suburbs."[2]

Table I documents statistically what may be seen in many cities as a trend leading to, and symptomatic of, our present urban distress.

TABLE I Population Changes in Newark, 1940–67

YEAR	TOTAL	WHITE		BLACK	
		NUMBER	PERCENT OF TOTAL	NUMBER	PERCENT OF TOTAL
1940	429,760	384,000	89.5	45,760	10.5
1950	438,776	363,149	82.9	74,965	17.1
1960	405,220	265,706	65.6	138,009	34.4
1967	398,000	158,000[1]	45.0	220,000	55.0

SOURCE: U.S. Bureau of the Census, 1940–60 and Social Agency projections for 1967.

[1] Including 20,000 Puerto Ricans.

[2] Newark, N. J.: New Jersey Historical Society, 1966, p. 298.

It will be noted that Newark moved from a typical American city of a white population preponderance in 1940 to one that had an estimated 47–65 percent black majority in 1967. These figures tell far more than a conventional analysis of change in ethnic group ratios might suggest. They are like the visible portion of an iceberg, the vast portion of which remains beneath the surface of the sea.

Newark's history has been marked by adjustments in power relations between British and German stock, and between the Italians, the Irish, and the Jews. Characteristically, however, black people have not entered fully into the power dynamics of the city's life. Every city is the same in this respect.

John Cunningham put his finger on the crucial difference in urban adjustment patterns of black newcomers to the city. He wrote: "Mistreatment of the Negro was clear by 1946, if politicians and business leaders had cared to acknowledge it. Equally, however, earnest volunteers, white and Negro, for many years had been working together to *solve problems of racial tension*." (Italics mine.)[3]

The emphasis has been upon solving the problems of racial "tension" rather than upon dealing with the crucial underlying factor of a relative powerlessness on the part of black people. This has been the most tragic aspect of urban life since World War II. Other ethnic groups entering our cities have shared aggressively in the power dynamics of city life. Uniquely, black men have been conditioned to take the stance of outsiders, or guests. Harsh circumstances during the 1910's and 1920's, and associated with the mass migration of black people to our cities, tended to force the behavior of black people into such an unfortunate mold.

Black people came to our cities for relief from oppressive conditions in the rural South. "Relief," in terms of a welfare-oriented marginal existence, is what the black newcomer found. (In 1960, 42 percent of the population of Newark had migrated from the South.) Unaccustomed to participation in even the most rudimentary aspects of the power dynamics of their communities of origin, these black newcomers brought with them an imposed history of defeatism and dependence. This seemed to fit well with

[3] *Ibid.*, p. 300.

the maintenance of the reigns of power by those who held nominal control.

Power is never freely shared, but only where there exist equitable relationships of power tension can the lot of the least fortunate be addressed in other than superficial ways. The immigration of black people to the heart of our nation's cities has been accompanied in a singular way by a failure to deal with the problems of equity and investment in city life and with the extension of the ability of the less fortunate to command answers to their own needs in self-directed ways.

Hence, the statistically increasing influx of black people into our urban centers has meant the statistically effective and potentially perilous addition of frustration and despair. This has created a vicious circle that now promises to become a whirlwind that will envelop the whole of the nation.

Black people who came to Newark during and after World War II found a state of disrepair characteristic of American cities. The postwar Newark into which these migrants came had been marked by a steady economic decline. Industries had been moving out and locating in more remote suburban regions. In 1909, for example, Newark's employment force represented 20 percent of that of the state of New Jersey. By 1939 the figure was down to 11 percent. Wages had moved from 25 percent of the state's total in 1909 to 10 percent in 1939. Between 1938 and 1944, industries left at such a pace as to represent a loss to the City of Newark of three hundred million dollars in assessed valuation.

Schools were in need of improvement. At least ten million dollars was needed for street repair. These conditions were reflective of a general neglect occasioned or intensified by wartime conditions. Typical of conditions faced by black arrivals was housing blight, with Newark's decaying slums among the worst in the nation. Nearly one-third of all the dwelling units in Newark in 1944 were reported to be below minimum standards of health and decency. Outhouses were still in use. Fires caused by defective burners and quickened in intensity by oil-soaked stairways made the characterless frame tenements of Newark's Central Ward in particular into a kind of living inferno. Those bereft of possessions and loved ones moved from place to place and, along with the fresh numbers of

TABLE II   Proportion of Negroes in the Thirty Largest U.S. Cities 1950, 1960, and Estimated 1965

	1950	1960	ESTIMATED[1] 1965
New York, New York	10	14	18
Chicago, Illinois	14	23	28
Los Angeles, California	9	14	17
Philadelphia, Pennsylvania	18	26	31
Detroit, Michigan	16	29	34
Baltimore, Maryland	24	35	38
Houston, Texas	21	23	23
Cleveland, Ohio	16	29	34
Washington, D.C.	35	54	66
St. Louis, Missouri	18	29	36
Milwaukee, Wisconsin	3	8	11
San Francisco, California	6	10	12
Boston, Massachusetts	5	9	13
Dallas, Texas	13	19	21
New Orleans, Louisiana	32	37	41
Pittsburgh, Pennsylvania	12	17	20
San Antonio, Texas	7	7	8
San Diego, California	5	6	7
Seattle, Washington	3	5	7
Buffalo, New York	6	13	17
Cincinnati, Ohio	16	22	24
Memphis, Tennessee	37	37	40
Denver, Colorado	4	6	9
Atlanta, Georgia	37	38	44
Minneapolis, Minnesota	1	2	4
Indianapolis, Indiana	15	21	23
Kansas City, Missouri	12	18	22
Columbus, Ohio	12	16	18
Phoenix, Arizona	5	5	5
Newark, New Jersey	17	34	47

SOURCE: U.S. Bureau of the Census.

[1] Except for Cleveland, Buffalo, Memphis, and Phoenix, for which a special census has been made in recent years, these are very rough estimations computed on the basis of the change in relative proportions of Negro births and deaths since 1960.

black arrivals, into increasingly crowded tenements. "Anyone who knew the city," John Cunningham wryly reports, "was aware that owners of slum property gouged these tenants mercilessly."

Table I indicates how the white population of the City of Newark moved rapidly downward from approximately 384,000 in 1940, to 363,000 in 1950, to 266,000 in 1960, and to an estimated 158,000 in 1967. Those who came to make up the preponderance of the population were largely black. Their population figures rose from approximately 46,000 in 1940, to 70,000 in 1950, to 125,000 in 1960 (plus 15,000 Puerto Ricans), and to an estimated 220,000 in 1967.

No typical American city has as yet experienced such a precipitous change from a white to a black majority. Washington, D.C., has a larger black population proportion, but its atypical circumstance as the capital of the nation creates a higher general educational level, greater opportunities for economic adjustment, and more governmental services designed to ameliorate the consequences of change. Nonetheless, Newark's predicament sug-

TABLE III Community Population, Newark, 1950–60

| | POPULATION | |
COMMUNITY	1960	1950
Forest Hill and Silver Lake	21,530	20,900
Roseville	28,816	29,200
West Ward	62,485	62,600
Central Ward	57,669	66,700
Clinton Hill	41,289	33,400
Weequahic-Dayton	41,451	54,200
Central Business District	12,914	12,500
South Broad	16,157	12,500
North Newark	43,243	45,900
Ironbound	43,586	50,100
Vailsburg	35,709	29,200
Meadowland	154	—
Total	405,003	417,200
CVR	217	
Grand Total	405,220	417,200

SOURCE: U.S. Bureau of the Census and *Urban Renewal Second Interim Report*, Newark, New Jersey.

gests the certain future of our major American cities. Table II provides a definite indication of this.

In the face of the precipitous black migration to Newark, the white population has moved in two directions. It has moved into the suburbs; and it has entrenched itself in several sections of the city.

Table III shows the adjustment of population by census tracts in the twelve recognized neighborhoods of the city.

WHITE ENTRENCHMENT

Seven of Newark's twelve neighborhoods have reflected a pattern of white entrenchment or a holding of the line against an "invasion" by the growing black population. These communities form almost a complete ring around the central core of Newark where the overwhelming majority of the city's black population resides.

An examination of the types of neighborhoods that have held the line, together with their patterns of population adjustment, should provide insight into the continuing process of frustration that the post-World War II mass entry of black people has entailed.

The communities where entrenchment against the extensive influx of black people has prevailed are: (1) Forest Hill–Silver Lake, (2) North Newark, (3) Roseville, (4) Vailsburg, (5) Ironbound, (6) Meadowland, and (7) Weequahic–Dayton Street.

Table IV shows the pattern of racial movement in Newark over a ten-year period.

1. **Forest Hill–Silver Lake.** The Forest Hill–Silver Lake community is situated at the northeast end of Newark. See Map I. Forest Hill is predominantly residential in character. It is Newark's most prestigious community, comprising "old first families" and an increasing number of families of Italian origin. The bulk of the city's spacious homes are in this community. The area contains well-maintained apartment buildings, some of which afford a highly prized commanding view of New York City's West Side skyline. Silver Lake, adjacent to Forest Hill, is predominantly Italian and chiefly made up of multiple-dwellings for clerks and tradesmen.

Between 1950 and 1960 the Forest Hill–Silver Lake community

TABLE IV Population Change by Census Tract, Newark, 1950–60

COMMUNITY	CENSUS TRACTS	TOTAL POPULATION 1960	TOTAL POPULATION 1950	WHITE POPULATION 1960	WHITE IN-CREASE	WHITE DE-CREASE	BLACK POPULATION 1950	BLACK POPULATION 1960	BLACK IN-CREASE	BLACK DE-CREASE
Forest Hill–Silver Lake	1	4,906	4,215	4,609	394		7	—		7
	2	1,987	1,963	1,476		487	500	511	11	
	3	3,039	4,012	2,711		1,301	179	328	149	
	4	1,952	2,162	1,819		343	166	133		33
	94	5,017	3,898	4,973	1,075		37	44	7	
	95	4,890	4,911	4,880		31	18	10		8
TOTAL		21,791	21,161	20,468	1,469	2,162	907	1,026	167	48
					−693				+119	
Roseville	5	1,441	1,551	1,405		146	38	36		2
	6	3,985	4,202	3,937		265	51	48		3
	7	5,447	5,725	5,367		358	13	80	67	
	8	3,837	3,816	3,487		329	314	350	36	
	9	5,048	5,537	4,589		948	29	459	430	
	10	3,396	3,243	2,511		732	236	885	649	
	16	5,622	5,397	3,845		1,552	717	1,777	1,060	
TOTAL		28,776	29,471	25,141		4,330	1,398	3,635	2,242	5
					−4,330				+2,237	

18

West Ward

13	3,648	3,035	1,741	1,294	1,157	1,907	750
14	5,334	5,461	3,893	1,568	46	1,441	1,395
15	3,999	3,477	1,508	1,969	613	2,491	1,878
17	4,868	3,271	1,361	1,910	1,841	3,507	1,666
18	4,289	4,492	3,368	1,124	182	921	739
26	3,873	4,117	3,568	549	25	305	280
27	3,772	3,946	2,300	1,646	102	1,472	1,370
28	1,847	2,229	1,632	597	23	215	192
29	4,137	4,115	2,234	1,881	378	1,903	1,525
32	4,559	4,298	2,074	2,224	201	2,485	2,284
33	4,220	3,932	1,838	2,094	252	2,382	2,130
34	3,230	3,327	2,468	859	18	762	744
35	2,927	3,134	2,878	256	7	49	42
36	3,300	3,535	3,064	471	9	236	227
37	2,667	2,724	1,330	1,394	33	1,337	1,304
38	5,614	4,139	1,334	2,805	1,308	4,280	2,972
TOTAL	62,284	58,232	36,591	−22,641	6,195	25,693	+19,498

TABLE IV Population Change by Census Tract, Newark, 1950-60—(Continued)

COMMUNITY	CENSUS TRACTS	TOTAL POPULATION 1960	WHITE POPULATION 1950	WHITE POPULATION 1960	WHITE INCREASE	WHITE DECREASE	BLACK POPULATION 1950	BLACK POPULATION 1960	BLACK INCREASE	BLACK DECREASE
Central Ward	11	3,247	2,394	1,162		1,232	1,511	2,085	574	
	12	3,940	1,977	545		1,432	2,311	3,395	1,084	
	30	3,876	2,065	502		1,563	3,186	3,374	188	
	31	5,428	2,520	751		1,769	1,407	4,677	3,270	
	39	3,552	1,828	553		1,275	2,463	2,999	536	
	60	3,890	893	265		628	4,123	3,625		498
	61	5,611	936	443		493	2,420	5,168	2,748	
	62	3,738	634	280		354	5,081	3,458		1,623
	63	2,543	641	135		506	3,116	2,408		708
	64	4,863	2,125	603		1,522	4,159	4,260	101	
	65	2,974	1,675	487		1,188	3,067	2,487		580
	66	4,707	1,074	578		496	5,587	4,129		1,458
	82	3,643	1,512	423		1,089	3,205	3,220	15	
	83	2,996	2,356	1,254		1,102	1,804	1,742		62
	84	2,546	2,340	1,252		1,088	1,018	1,294	276	
TOTAL		57,554	24,970	9,233		-15,737	44,458	48,321	8,792	4,929
										+3,863

20

Clinton Hill								
40	4,700	3,301	529	2,772	1,326	4,171	2,845	
41	4,652	4,315	1,933	2,382	28	2,719	2,691	
42	4,455	4,737	3,585	1,152	4	870	866	
52	3,048	3,391	2,470	921	25	578	553	
53	4,503	4,656	3,730	926	12	773	761	
54	6,385	6,293	2,134	4,159	229	4,251	4,022	
55	4,162	3,525	835	2,690	342	3,327	2,985	
56	3,932	3,116	668	2,448	320	3,264	2,944	
58	5,336	4,333	1,761	2,572	514	3,575	3,061	
TOTAL	41,173	37,667	17,645	−20,022	2,800	23,528	+20,728	
Weequahic-Dayton St.								
43	3,996	4,498	3,784	714	26	212	186	
44	2,852	3,083	2,806	277	18	46	28	
45	4,890	5,446	4,890	556	16	—		16
46	3,539	4,227	3,530	697	5	9	4	
47	4,606	5,000	4,591	409	31	15		16
48a }	8,875	8,720	1,622	2,773	663	1,811	2,265	
48b }			4,325	—	—	1,117		
49	4,165	4,710	4,024	686	16	141	125	
50	4,010	3,701	1,004	2,697	423	3,006	2,583	
51	4,410	4,579	2,782	1,797	29	1,628	1,599	
TOTAL	41,343	43,964	33,358	−10,606	1,227	7,985	6,790	32

$$+6,758$$

TABLE IV Population Change by Census Tract, Newark, 1950-60—(Continued)

COMMUNITY	CENSUS TRACTS	TOTAL	WHITE				BLACK			
		POPU-LATION 1960	POPU-LATION 1950	POPU-LATION 1960	IN-CREASE	DE-CREASE	POPU-LATION 1950	POPU-LATION 1960	IN-CREASE	DE-CREASE
Central Business District	80	3,136	3,059	1,516		1,543	1,502	1,620	118	
	81	4,157	3,104	1,463		1,641	2,541	2,694	153	
	85	5,426	5,874	3,587		2,287	1,041	1,839	798	
TOTAL		12,719	12,037	6,566		−5,471	5,084	6,153	+1,069	
South Broad St.	57	5,564	4,104	1,890		2,214	2,130	3,674	1,544	
	59	5,732	4,678	1,815		2,863	950	3,917	2,967	
	67	4,810	4,803	3,174		1,629	578	1,636	1,058	
TOTAL		16,106	13,585	6,879		−6,706	3,658	9,227	+5,569	
North Newark	86	4,597	3,379	2,562		817	2,254	2,035		219
	87	4,609	5,714	4,168		1,546	139	441	302	
	88	5,725	3,946	4,443	497		528	1,282	754	
	89	3,007	3,504	2,596		908	289	411	122	
	90	1,466	3,355	1,280		2,075	346	186		160
	91	3,428	3,871	3,342		529	159	86		73
	92	4,431	4,545	3,882		663	195	549	354	
	93	4,481	4,370	4,362		8	27	119	92	
	96	6,880	3,448	4,428	980		1,231	2,452	1,221	
	97	4,433	4,762	4,418		344	51	15		36
TOTAL		43,057	40,894	35,481	1,477	6,890	5,219	7,576	2,845	488
						−5,413				+2,357

Ironbound									
68	3,888	3,871	2,667		1,204	1,154	1,221	67	164
69	3,473	3,436	2,852		584	785	621		27
70	3,529	4,020	3,510		510	46	19		6
71	2,799	3,403	2,799		604	6	–		6
72	3,656	3,916	3,356		560	6	–		
73	3,353	3,722	3,255		467	9	98	89	
74	1,889	2,464	1,886		578	3	3		
75a	4,716	9,638	3,697		2,524	766	1,019	962	
75b	4,126		3,417		–		709		
76	2,174	2,836	1,971		865	263	203		60
77	2,787	3,395	2,778		617	30	9		21
78	3,114	3,168	2,798		370	329	316		13
79	4,277	4,033	3,926		107	416	351		65
TOTAL	35,548 43,781	47,902	38,912		−8,990	3,813	4,569	1,118	362
								+756	
Vailsburg									
19	2,935	3,864	2,748		1,116	105	187	82	
20	4,174	3,935	4,171	236	117	4	3		1
21	3,799	3,915	3,798			2	1		1
22	11,008	5,944	10,943	4,999		48	65	17	
23	4,499	4,535	4,499		36	1	–		
24	4,284	4,710	4,280		430	1	4	3	1
25	4,849	5,057	4,840		217	13	9		4
TOTAL	35,548	31,960	35,279	5,235	1,916	174	269	102	7
				+3,319				+95	
Newark Airport									
98	153	236	153		83	65	–		65
TOTAL	153	236	153		−83	65	–	0	−65

23

MAP I

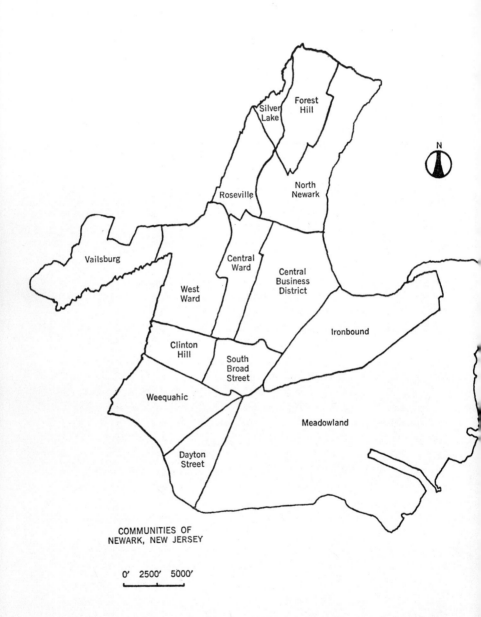

COMMUNITIES OF
NEWARK, NEW JERSEY

0' 2500' 5000'

SOURCE: From a base map prepared by the Newark Central Planning Board, October 1959.

experienced a decline in population of approximately six hundred. Approximately seven hundred white persons left the area, and a little more than one hundred black people were added to the population. Relatively this neighborhood tended to be stable. Overt and covert housing restrictions made it difficult for black people to buy homes or to gain access to rental or long-term lease apartments. With 95.06 percent of its people white and 4.77 percent black, Forest Hill–Silver Lake has the third lowest proportion of black people of any community in the city.

The Forest Hill section pays the highest taxes per dwelling unit of any area of Newark. It has the city's highest level of educational attainment. The bulk of the traditional leadership potential remaining in Newark is to be found in Forest Hill. A small colony of residences of the clergy of Newark's leading churches has long been established there. On many counts, Forest Hill should have been giving the City of Newark, in its period of mounting crisis, the wisdom associated with its acquired competencies and historical experience. Yet the area diminished in overall population as the post-World War II years proceeded, and the needed voices of its people were scarcely heard.

Escapism has been a growing mark of central city life. It spells peril, as problems mount with increasing numbers of so-called problem people left behind to find answers for themselves to inherited, as well as newly created, needs.

As school problems have grown, and as housing, sanitation, health, and welfare needs have soared, so also have Newark's taxes —but with a decreasing expectancy of good returns. In 1964 our family, for example, inspected a nine-room house in the Forest Hill section of Newark. It was situated on a 50 by 75-foot lot. The house was listed for 60 percent of the asking price of the twelve-room house we subsequently purchased in the nearby suburban section of Orange. But the taxes on the Newark house were more than double the taxes on the Orange property, which has nearly a quarter of an acre of land. Small wonder that some people move from the city! In some glaring instances, only those who can afford to live in the city remain. Yet those who have lived in the Forest Hill-type sections of Newark—and of every major city in the nation —should be exercising leadership in helping to face with frankness the seeming impossibilities that have made for mounting crisis.

Those who bury their heads in the sand cannot at the same time be sensitive to their own immediate survival needs. While successful in keeping a substantial proportion of aspiring black men of accomplishment and leadership potential from making their home in Forest Hill, other elements have quietly entered. Hence, the most shocking sex enterprise in Newark's recent history was disclosed to be located in the city's most fashionable and enlightened community of Forest Hill.

Forest Hill represents a fundamental problem facing every major city in America. How can diversity in life and leadership be developed and maintained for the regeneration of our central cities? Escapism and entrenchment thus far have failed; for only through death does flight cure any ill.

2. **North Newark.** North Newark is located east and south of the Forest Hill–Silver Lake area. An Italian population is concentrated in this area. The presence of two low-income public housing projects and the city's first large middle-to-high income redevelopment project make for considerable population mixture. North Newark's population decreased by more than 2,600 between 1950 and 1960. The white population experienced a decrease of 5,413. The black population increased from 5,219 in 1950 to 7,576 in 1960. Doubtless the white population tended to be stabilized by the addition of public housing units at the northern and southern ends of North Newark. However, both the public and private developments were ostensibly open to all. The predisposition on the part of black people with higher incomes to buy property for owner-occupancy or to live in owner-occupied multiple dwellings lessens the movement of middle and higher income black people into the large middle and higher income developments, such as the Colonnade Apartments in North Newark. In 1960 North Newark had an 82.05 percent white majority and a 17.60 percent black minority.

North Newark has represented a loss in owner-occupied homes. Single family homes have been converted to multiple dwellings. A Roman Catholic population of first- and second-generation foreign-born has increased, as white Protestants have fled the area. Growing black congregations, with membership from both Newark and the suburbs, have occupied property formerly owned by white Protestant churches.

One may travel along North Broadway, North Newark's major thoroughfare, and readily sense something of the growing tragedy that is called Newark. Fine-faced properties show the glaring signs of rapidly increasing decay. North Newark, as a whole, shows promise of precipitous dislocation and deterioration. Yet other areas claim a far higher priority on Newark's hoped-for resources for restoration. The most disheartening aspect of North Newark's life is the growing air of untidiness indicative of the presence of a people who feel they have no hope.

At the in-town end of North Newark, and adjacent both to Forest Hill and to Branch Brook, the city's most extensive and attractive park, is the middle-income housing development known as the Colonnades. The Colonnade Apartments represent the city's major attempt to bring largely white middle-income families back into the City of Newark. Financially the investment has been a failure. This fact undoubtedly will be underscored by the fresh encouragement of white flight from the city by the open warfare and massacre in Newark's streets this past summer.

No one likes living in or near an armed camp. People seek a setting of tranquility for their hours of rest. This is not promised in a city where, in the face of overcrowded classrooms with double shifts, a third of a million dollars was spent in the late summer of 1967 alone on barbed wire, armored vehicles, and weapons of assault and human destruction. When a group of citizens of the nearby community of Verona were asked what they disliked most about the open rebellion in Newark, their principal reply was that they disliked the sight of patrol wagons passing through their municipality bearing the arrested to the county jail!

More Colonnade Apartments will not bring more white people back to the city permanently. We may even question, far more seriously than in the past, the wisdom or worthiness of this goal. Does the city need the infusion of white people per se? Or does the city need to find and use any and all reasonable means to facilitate the capacity for self-directed achievement on the part of those who choose freely to remain or to return? For the moment, let us postpone the answer. Let it suffice for us to ponder at least the propriety of many of our former goals.

3. Roseville. Also in the northern extension of Newark is the

Roseville community. Its population is diverse. The area has a substantial core of business institutions and residences. Roseville experienced an overall population decrease of slightly less than 400 between 1950 and 1960. The white population decreased from 29,471 in 1950 to 25,141 in 1960. The black population increased from 1,398 in 1950 to 3,635 in 1960. Thus Roseville has remained predominantly white, with an 87.25 percent white majority and a 12.61 percent black minority.

With its three-family houses and several broad tree-lined streets immediately adjacent to an area of black preponderence, Roseville seems to be a logical area for mounting black population invasion. Roseville has a quiet, semisuburban air about it, even though its fringes, notably along Orange Street, are noisy and show the signs of encroaching blight. Several spacious and largely empty white Protestant churches retain a semblance of its once nearly arrived at splendor. Peck House, a lovely mansion situated on property that is bounded on three sides by Sussex Avenue and North Fifth and North Sixth Streets, also reflects a Newark that once was. Tenements face Peck House on every side and speak silently of the strangeness of beauty in the midst of the amorphous ugliness that characterizes Newark. Again this represents today what most major central cities will soon be like. Newark's suburban communities, with spacious lawns and well-kept homes, with affluent and well-trained people, are incorporated municipalities. Politically and civically they are unrelated to the central city where their people's livelihood is earned.

The half-empty churches and the more than 87 percent white majority in Roseville in 1960 speak of a universal urge that must be faced with frankness if our cities are to provide the ground for untroubled and harmonious change. People feel that their institutions are extensions of themselves. Whether public or private, whatever institutions have been associated with their group's past life people come to feel "belong" to them and to those whom they feel are most nearly related to them. While newcomers may be welcomed into schools, hospitals, churches, and other agencies, the perceptions and experiences of a lifetime tend to create a persistent partition between the old and the new, between those who belong on the one hand and the outsiders on the other hand who are, at best, forever one's guests. As continuing and accelerating change itself becomes our clearest constant, the Rosevilles of America raise the question of how self-preservation may be accomplished without the unconscious building in of the suicide toward which our cities are headed, with their present thoughtless patterns of in-group entrenchment. See Table V.

TABLE V   Population Change by Location, Inside and Outside Metropolitan Areas, 1950–66 (Numbers in Millions)

| | POPULATION | | | | | |
| | BLACK | | | WHITE | | |
	1950	1960	1966	1950	1960	1966
United States	15.0	18.8	21.5	135.2	158.8	170.8
Metropolitan areas	8.4	12.2	14.8	80.3	99.7	109.0
Central cities	6.5	9.7	12.1	45.5	47.7	46.4
Urban fringe	1.9	2.5	2.7	34.8	52.0	62.5
Smaller cities, towns, and rural	6.7	6.7	6.7	54.8	59.2	61.8

| | CHANGE, 1950–66 | | | |
| | BLACK | | WHITE | |
	NUMBER	PERCENT	NUMBER	PERCENT
United States	6.5	43	35.6	26
Metropolitan areas	6.4	77	28.7	36
Central cities	5.6	87	9	2
Urban fringe	.8	42	27.7	79
Smaller cities, towns, and rural	Z[1]	1	7.0	13

[1] Z Rounds to less than 500,000.
SOURCE: U.S. Bureau of the Census.

Planning instruments, whereby all segments of city life may share in continuous and enlightened planning in significant and structured ways, are the most basic need in every major American city. Planning of various kinds has been done. But the absence, for example, of crucial planning by black people as a whole for clearly black needs, even as we would have planning by merchants for merchants' needs, suggests that we have not extended as we might all of the reasonable limits of our urban planning dynamics.

4. **Vailsburg.** Jutting like a finger pointing westward out of Newark and into the midst of the adjacent suburbs is the Vailsburg community. Vailsburg, with a 98.80 percent white majority and a .75 percent black minority has the smallest proportion of black people of any community in Newark. Families of Irish origin predominate, followed by those of Italian origin. The Mayor's residence and the homes of a large number of city officials are situated in this community. At the far western end of Vailsburg, and contiguous with the towns of South Orange and Maplewood, and the cities of East Orange and Irvington, is Ivy Hill, the newest residential section of the city.

The Ivy Hill area of Vailsburg covers census tract 22. Its total population in 1950 was 5,999. In 1960 it had increased 85.76 percent to 11,144, representing 5,145 new persons living in this area. Of this number in 1950, 48 were black. By 1960, the black population had increased by 35.42 percent, representing 17 new persons and making a total of 65.

It must be noted that this represented the second largest increase in black population by census tract in Vailsburg. The greatest increase in black population occurred in census tract 19 at the in-town or extreme eastern end of the community. This area is almost wholly separated from the rest of Vailsburg by the Garden State Parkway. Tract 19, with a total population of 3,975 in 1950, experienced a 26.2 percent decrease to 2,935 in 1960. This represented a loss of a little more than 1,000 persons. The black population of tract 19 moved from 105 in 1950 to 187 in 1960. The 78.10 percent increase represented a numerical change of only 82.

Meanwhile, census tract 20 experienced a decrease in black population from 4 to 3. Tract 22 decreased from 2 to 1. Tract 23 lost its only black inhabitant. Tract 24 increased its black population from 1 to 4, and tract 25 decreased its black population from 13 to 9. Clearly Vailsburg reflected a pattern of white entrenchment against the growing trend to be seen elsewhere in Newark toward black invasion and succession.

Vailsburg represents, in the most clear and aggressive way, the kind of urban escapism that makes for doom. Not only is it the place of residence of a substantial number of Irish and Italian officials in city government, it is also reported to be the domicile of much of the leadership of organized crime.

The low-level, unsophisticated, power-grasping politician syndrome, far too often found in our cities today, was reflected unconsciously in a telephone interview with one of the chief assistants to the Mayor of Newark. Periodically, I write to the Mayor of Newark indicating my willingness to be of service to him and his administration. Only once did I receive a formal reply, and it was by telephone. The conversation went like this: "Dr. Wright, a file is being kept here in our office on you. We appreciate your interest but we note that your name was mentioned in the paper several times in conjunction with the Newark Committee for Better Public Schools. Now, frankly, we consider this group. . . . Also , we notice that your picture was taken with. . . . To be quite honest with you, we consider him to be a political enemy. . . ."

The mind that sees only the "good guys" and the "bad guys," the cronies and the agitators, is one foreign to the best interests, and alien to the basic traditions of our nation's life. Assuredly the Mayor of Newark would not knowingly condone such an administrative approach. Nonetheless, it finds an unfortunate place in Newark and other cities.

All newcomers to America's shores potentially provide rich and ready resources for national fulfillment. However, there must be growth into new world ways and growth out of the tired and unfruitful old world ways that have impelled many of our people to cast anchor here. The eminent and certainly noncontroversial urbanist and population scholar, Dr. Philip Hauser, of the University of Chicago, writes of this situation in the following way:

This nation has been characterized not only by tremendous rates of population growth and of urbanization and metropolitanization but, also, by great heterogeneity of population, by diverse ethnic, cultural, religious, and racial groups. It is small wonder that we are still learning how to live in our new physical and social milieu and with each other. This nation contains virtually every level of pre-urban and urban and metropolitan culture, many diverse and often conflicting attitudes and ideologies and many varied and often conflicting forms of behavior. Furthermore, this nation contains many newcomers, white and nonwhite, who are still in the process of acculturation or Americanization.

They still possess greatly varying value systems including myths and twisted and distorted stereotypes including ethnic and racial stereotypes. Many of our newcomers, including 19th and 20th century white immigrants, still do not understand and certainly have not accepted the ideology and the ideals of the American Constitutional system and cultural heritage, let alone an understanding of its implications for life in the 20th century world.[4]

The Americanization of those who reside in our cities is crucial to urban regeneration as well as to national fulfillment. Perhaps the accelerated emphasis upon the alleged cultural deprivation of black Americans is in part another effectively escapist mechanism for those who find it too difficult to face our staggering urban needs.

(Educational instruments—with built-in status and rewards— need to be devised for an entire adult population in order to equip our adults for a world of continuing change. The untutored, the unsophisticated, the unself-directed, make up an increasingly substantial proportion of the electorate. A society cannot become or remain free, unless its voters' minds are freed to make free choices. Power joined with ignorance is the mother of presumption. This is no adequate base either for urban regeneration or for our survival as a free people. The people of the Vailsburgs, along with those of the black heartland of Newark and elsewhere, need to be exposed continually and in depth to the liberating arts and disciplines that make men truly free. New urban adult educational instruments, for those fully employed and for those who must become employed, need to be provided for by federal mandate and at federal expense (for they are the only enterprise equipped to do so) or we as a nation cannot hope to survive.[5])

5. The Ironbound. Situated at the eastern end of Newark and hemmed in by railroads, a river, and the largely uninhabitable meadowland is the community known as the Ironbound. The Ironbound consists of a lower-middle-class population with old but well-kept brick and frame multiple dwellings, a relatively large

[4] *Renewal*, September 1967, p. 20.
[5] See discussion of the needed role for a federally financed, authentic community college system designed to meet a broad range of adult requirements in my *Black Power and Urban Unrest: Creative Possibilities* (N.Y., Hawthorne Books, 1967).

number of which are owner-occupied. The community is characterized as the "melting-pot" in the city and is essentially stable. It
contains a high mixture of land uses, with industries chiefly on
its fringes.

The total population of the Ironbound decreased from 50,100 in
1950 to 43,586 in 1960. The black population of approximately
3,800 in 1950 decreased by 300 to approximately 3,500 in 1960.
The white population decreased during the same decade by a
little more than 4,000. In 1960 the Ironbound was 89.28 percent
white and 10.46 percent black. This so-called "melting pot" is
in actuality a network of ethnic neighborhoods, all accommodat-
ing themselves in varying ways to the presence and needs of
others.

There is a deep lesson for our cities in a community such as the
Ironbound. The "melting-pot" conception, as practiced in reference to all rising ethnic groups, has not meant a lack of group co-
hesiveness, save for those who are black. There has always been
enforced integration in all public relationships between Poles and
Italians, between British and Irish, yet never as an end in itself.
The effective public desegregation of these groups meant an aggressive clearing of the slate so that all might have the fullest access
to common opportunity as long as the rudimentary rights of all
were kept intact.

Ethnocentrism, or the glorification of one's primary racial or
ethnic group of reference, is the most basic and pervasive of all
social traits. Yet in our cities black self-awareness has been looked
upon and treated as though it were an evil to be shunned. It is
this missing personal and group pride and self-awareness that
breeds self-hate and that allows men to develop an active disregard
for the person and property of others.

Group identification provides the foundation for personal identity. All men need to have a positive sense of their groups of primary reference. The stages in growth toward involvement in our
common humanity are first, group pride (pride of race or ances-
tral nation, based in no small part on mythology); second, personal
self-awareness in conformity to the role model of the ethnic group;
third, larger identifications based upon the aggressive sense of one's
worth as developed in stages one and two. To omit stage one is

to heighten the faulty development of an already far too long benighted group.

The solidarity of a group affords its members the permanent privilege of two choices. It allows one to have the option of emphasizing those relationships of primary identification. It enables one to move into other relationships with pride, status, dignity, and the support of group power.

So it may well be fortuitous that black people have been caught at this particular juncture in the cities. Unutilized for good, they have portended evil and disaster. Recognized for its potential worth, black pride born of the latent power of black group proximity may become the single most vital ingredient in the regeneration of urban life.

6. The Meadowland.   The Meadowland area of Newark is represented by census tract 97. It comprises one-fourth of the land area of the city and contains the Newark Airport and Port Newark. The remainder of the Meadowland is almost wholly presently uninhabitable marshland. In 1950 the meadowland's population was 301. Of this number 236 were white; 65 were black. In 1960 the total population had decreased to 154. The black population had disappeared.

The Meadowland area of Newark represents urban desolation at its very worst. Yet other cities may come to experience blight of no less excellence. The Meadowlands stand as a stark reminder that blind localism has, in our day, passed its reasonable limits. Newark needs the Meadowlands, which might add more than 10 percent to its tax base and to its useful land area for beautification and for the relaxation of population pressures. Only the nation as a whole has the resources to reclaim the Meadowland. Only the nation as a whole may restore wholeness to our increasingly distraught cities.

Clearly our emphasis must be upon new national interrelationships. Intrastate metropolitan regions—a growing phenomenon in urban America—can function efficiently only through national facilitation. The losses and the gains accrue to the nation. It seems strange, indeed, that the country which considers itself the most enlightened in the world is the only advanced nation that has not unburdened itself of the medieval fetish of localism.

Localism represents a form of civic immaturity that cannot give even a little in order to receive the gifts of life, health, and the possibility of growth into fulfillment. It is a manifestation of the same mind that misreads American history to prize the neighborhood school, knowing full well that many of our grandparents who walked miles on end to school would have been grateful for buses. This does not, in itself, defend the practice of bussing for the supposed benefit of black pupils' learning, but in an age of increased sophistication, more than simple geography should provide the groundwork for social and civic choices.

7. **Weequahic-Dayton Street.** The Weequahic section of Newark is a comfortable historically Jewish section of the city. In attractiveness it ranks second only to Forest Hill. And like Forest Hill its fine residences are situated in a relatively narrow strip, at the edge of which the quality and attractiveness of the area decrease sharply. Handsome homes in Newark are a scarce commodity; spacious lawns are practically nonexistent. The typical homesite in the Weequahic area, for example is no more than 60 by 80 feet.

Weequahic contains several Jewish-oriented retail and commercial sections and Newark's second largest park, bearing the same name as the community. The Dayton Street section of the Weequahic-Dayton Street "neighborhood" is somewhat isolated from the rest of the city. The Meadowlands' Weequahic Park and major transportation lines make the Dayton Street area almost a community apart. It consists of two public housing projects and a number of one to six family structures. The Dayton Street School is the major institution in the area.

The Dayton Street area comprises census tract 48B. In 1950 this area was combined with census tract 48A in the Weequahic section and was designated census tract 48. This makes it difficult to report accurately on the shift in racial composition of the Dayton Street area. It can be noted, however, that the black population of the combined area increased by more than two thousand between 1950 and 1960, while the white population for the area decreased by nearly three thousand.

The more suburban Weequahic area reflected a pattern of invasion and succession in the three tracts, 48A, 50, and 51, mentioned previously. Succession is the condition of substantial change or adjustment in population preponderance, while invasion reflects no more than a significant entry by a new group into an area.

Census tract 50 had a black population of 423 out of a total of 4,143 in 1950. Black people had clearly made a significant entry into the tract area, representing more than 10 percent of the total population. Tract area 51 in 1950 had a black population of 29 out of a total population of 4,611. This represented only between one-half and three-quarters of one percent of the population.

By 1960 tract area 50 had experienced an increase of 2,583 blacks and a decrease of 2,697 whites. The black population in 1960 thus represented 65 percent of census tract 50. Tract area 51 had experienced between 1950 and 1960 a change in black population proportion from .75 percent to 40 percent. Succession had been accomplished in census tract 50; it had been all but accomplished in census tract 51. Census tracts 48A, 50, and 51 are situated at the in-town end of Weequahic, away from the peripheral areas which—throughout the city—have tended to be reflective of white entrenchment.

The remaining census tracts in Weequahic represent the same clear pattern of a slow entry or exclusion of black people as was apparent in the other areas that ring the city. Tract 43, with a total population of 4,524 in 1950, had lost 528 persons by 1960, making a total of 3,996. One hundred and eight-six black people were added; 714 white were lost. Whites were leaving faster than blacks were entering.

Tract 44, with a total population of 3,102 in 1950, had decreased in 1960 to 2,852, representing a total loss of 250. Two hundred and seventy-seven white people had left the area at the same time as 28 blacks made their entry, bringing the black population of tract 44 to 46 persons.

Tract 45, in 1950, had a population of 5,462. In 1960 these numbers had decreased to 4,892. Meanwhile 556 whites had left the area. The entire black population, however, numbering 16 in 1950, had disappeared.

Tract 46 had a population of 4,234 in 1950. Between 1950 and 1960 this number was diminished by 667, leaving 3,567 persons in the area. The black population of 5 in 1950 moved upward to nine in 1960.

Tract 47 represented a total population of 5,033 in 1950 and 4,610 in 1960. In the ten-year interval 423 persons had left the area. The black population had decreased from 31 to 15.

Tract 49 had a total population of 4,730 in 1950. This had decreased to 4,175 in 1960, with an overall loss of 555. The black population moved from 16 to 141, representing a gain of 125. In 1960 the Weequahic-Dayton Street Community had been successful in holding the line. Of the community, 80.48 percent was still white as the black masses were pressing even harder to reach the city's semisuburban borders.

The Weequahic section of Newark, like practically every community in Newark, reflects pervasive problems, needs, challenges, and opportunities to be found in the life of our cities. It demonstrates that for some who live in Newark pride still reigns. In spite of a diminishing Jewish population, handsome new religious and business structures have recently been built by the Jewish community. Riding through Weequahic, one gets the feeling that while others may abandon the central city, at least some are here to stay.

Yet the Jewish community is expanding into the near and more remote suburbs. Temple B'nai Jeshrun, outside the Weequahic community, provides a case in point. The Newark headquarters for the congregation is one of the most imposing religious structures in Newark. B'nai Jeshrun has a suburban synagogue extension and school in the exceptionally affluent municipality of South Orange. It has also built a magnificent new synagogue near the Short Hills line in Livingston. The Jewish community, at least in some respects in Essex County, seems to have reached out to include both the central city and the suburbs in the embrace of its concerns.

But the Jewish community in Weequahic exhibits, in a helpful way, some dynamics of which those who are responsible in our cities must be fully aware. The Jewish community has befriended black people far beyond its proportions in the total concern shown by white people for those in Newark who are black. Names like Samuel Convissor, formerly with the Greater Newark Development Council and now administrator in the community relations office of RCA, and of Nadeline Dworkin and Jack Mayers of the Newark Committee for Better Public Schools would give the record of any city, for its efforts at facilitating power for the powerless, a more clearly brilliant luster. The list of such names could go on and on.

But the most recent election for councilman from the ward of which Weequahic is a part reflected a vote along almost solidly ethnic lines. The Jewish community voted for the Jewish candidate. The black community voted for the black candidate. There being more white voters than black, the Jewish candidate won. And look at the victorious councilman. He has been against measures for school improvement suggested by the Newark Committee for Better Public Schools. He is one of several councilmen, along with the councilman from Vailsburg, who have been intractable in their insistence upon the use of police dogs in the streets of Newark. This councilman's record seems to be the most reactionary and repressive in the present Newark City Council.

Black people, not having a tradition of entering fully into the power dynamics of our cities, have tended to judge others outside their community in terms of friend or foe. When only relief is asked, this does make a vital difference, but in power politics it is beside the point and gratuitous to make such a value judgment. It is appropriate only to decide what positive coalition will provide the power for one's own progress, as it is bound up with the progress of the city.

(The overall result has been that the communities at the extreme northern, southern, and western ends of the city have tended to hold the line against an influx of growing numbers of black people from within. The remaining central portion of the city has been left to absorb the swelling numbers of black migrants. We may trace the pattern of that absorption as it reveals the growing symptoms of civic distress.)

"THE ROTTEN CASKET"

The distinguished Chairman of the Newark Commission for Human Rights, Albert Black, once spoke of the black core area of Newark as "the rotten casket destined for the burial of the living dead." The black slums of Newark reflect patterns of life typical of black slums throughout America. The continued existence of these "rotten caskets" holds the promise of disaster. Indeed, the state of mind that produced them has divided the nation in almost apartheid fashion. Black people sense their containment as hostile aggression against them. Ralph Bunche thus explained, "The ghettos of America are like the native reserves in South Africa. They symbolize the Negro as unacceptable, inferior, and therefore, kept apart."

The so-called "rotten casket" areas of black containment in Newark are (1) the Central Ward, (2) the West Ward, (3) Clinton Hill, (4) the Central Business District, and (5) South Broad Street.

The names themselves reflect the lack of character of the black core areas of Newark, as compared to such names as Roseville, Forest Hill, Silver Lake, Vailsburg, and Weequahic. See Map II.

1. The Central Ward. The black heartland of Newark is known as the Central Ward. It is in most respects a typical big city black slum. The Newark Central Planning Board, in its study "Newark, A City in Transition", wrote of the Central Ward in 1962: "The city's worst slums are located in the southern end of this neighborhood. However, it is now undergoing a major redevelopment. There are two existing public housing projects, another under construction, and one in the planning. The population is predominantly Negro."

Let us look at the Central Ward in the light of this bland statement. The population of the Central Ward in 1950 was 66,700; in 1960 it had decreased to 57,669, representing a loss of 9,000 persons. The white population moved downward from 25,000 in 1950 to 8,200 in 1960, representing a loss of approximately 16,800 persons. The black population of the Central Ward moved downward from approximately 49,000 in 1950 to approximately 42,000 in 1960. The community is characterized by large areas of vacated land and has the city's largest proportion of unfit dwellings marked for demolition. Currently more than 20,000 persons are scheduled to be displaced for the already mentioned medical-dental college complex during a period of several years. For more than twenty

MAP II Community Composition Percent Negro and White 1960

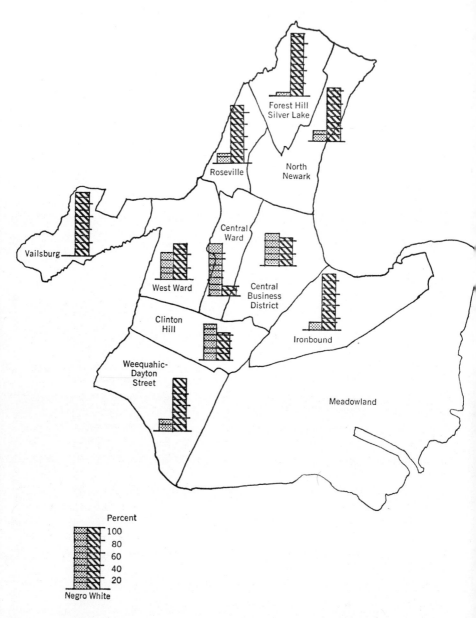

SOURCE: From a base map prepared by the Newark Central Planning Board, December 1960.
SOURCE: U.S. Bureau of the Census, 1960.

years the Central Ward has been the temporary refuge for black people in a state of prolonged "transition."

Table VI shows the numerical and percentage changes in population by census tract areas.

TABLE VI   Population Shift Pattern in the Central Ward, Newark, 1950–60

CENSUS TRACT	NUMERICAL CHANGE		PERCENT OF CHANGE	
	INCREASE	DECREASE	INCREASE	DECREASE
11		650		16.63
12		343		8.00
30		1,376		26.17
31	1,490		37.84	
39		730		17.00
60		1,040		22.66
61	2,271		67.61	
62		1,974		34.49
63		1,214		32.49
64		1,418		22.53
65		1,768		37.23
66		1,962		29.39
82		1,068		22.61
83		1,170		28.07
84		804		23.93

Only two census tracts gained in overall population. Effectively the area was being stripped of its inhabitants. Persons displaced for the new housing units are reported by the Newark Housing Authority to move near the area from which they have been removed. As a result, the Central Ward tends to be an area in perpetual motion. The high pupil turnover rate for the city, 44 percent in 1965, underscores this same trend.

In spite of having the highest rate of dwelling unit demolition, the Central Ward had, in 1960, the largest number of inhabited dwelling units of any community in the city. In 1960 there were 19,369 dwelling units in the Central Ward. Of these, 7,656 were reported sound, while 6,772 were reported to be deteriorating and 4,941 were reported to be dilapidated. This suggests the certain future for increased population movement within the Central Ward. In 1960 the Central Ward was 83.79 percent black, and 16.01 percent white.

The equivalent of Newark's Central Ward is called by its own special name in every city. But whether it's a Watts, a South Side, a Harlem, a Bedford-Stuyvesant, a West End, a Hill, a Hollow, or a "Down the way," the plight in terms of the desecration of human life is still the same.

Passing along the New Jersey Turnpike east of Newark, a small girl took notice of Newark's skyline as it rose just beyond the marshland. The strange, soft, red box-shaped buildings that dominated a portion of the skyline were especially intriguing. She asked her mother: "What are those buildings that look like boxes?" "A city project," the mother answered, and the girl said: "Oh, I know what you mean, Mother, a city jail!"

Had the inquirer been several miles closer, she would have understood more clearly the uncanny wisdom of her seemingly innocent remark. The public housing projects of the nation, by and large, are like semisanitary dungeons that make men feel they are less than men. Visit almost any public housing project in any central city. Visit them in the Central Ward of Newark. Their cold uniform ugliness and sometimes their unkemptness are almost enough to condemn them as unworthy of the spirit of man. Public housing in the Central Ward is semisanitized slum property built and maintained at the expense of the tax-paying public. As a nursery leader in a housing unit in the Central Ward, my wife was forced for a time to rearrange the classroom furnishings in order that she might see the rats entering the classroom before the children had a chance to see them.

The Central Wards of the nation tend to keep their tenants as wards. They breed drug and welfare addiction and are the proving ground for irresponsibility and despair. Our antipoverty program officials are learning that the total environment or way of life of the black heartlands of the cities militates against any piecemeal efforts that fail to deal with the built-in problems of self-hate and desperation born of powerlessness to control even the basic immediacies of one's own life-situation.

Those who live in the Central Wards of our cities have sensed all too well that in our society, however noisy our declarations, power is more to be respected than people. Those in our central cities need to discover and to exercise the residual power at their command. They need power, however, not as poor people but as black people. It is the low status and the state of general powerlessness of black people as a whole that accounts for the lion's share of the disparity between black and white income as documented by Table VII. Hence, broad black coalitions, representing every segment of the black community, are called for to deal with the black problem as a whole. Only then may the poverty aspect of a basically black problem be addressed in an unself-defeating way.

TABLE VII   Influence of Number of Earners on Family Income, 1966

	ALL FAMILIES	NO EARNERS	ONE EARNER	TWO EARNERS	THREE EARNERS (OR MORE)
Negro:					
Percent	100	10	35	40	15
Median income	$4,463	$1,914	$3,728	$5,652	$6,583
White:					
Percent	100	8	43	36	13
Median income	$7,722	$2,358	$6,877	$8,801	$11,464
Negro median income as a percent of white	58	81	54	64	57

SOURCE: U.S. Bureau of the Census.

⟨I live in suburban Orange, New Jersey, on the border line of the highly affluent village of South Orange. The neighborhood is effectively segregated. It is practically all-white. Our presence does not integrate the neighborhood; for in a strict sense it is an area where few know each other but all share the attractive physical environment. When asked why I do not live in the ghetto, my answer is that the question is loaded. I *do* live in the ghetto. The ghetto is present where every black man in America lives. Black people—by sharing in the corporate assessment presently placed on blackness in America—are tied together by a common condition of low status and high vulnerability in a white controlled and historically racist world. If one is black in America, one's fortunes are inextricably interwoven with those of its Central Wards. The presence of a delusion among some few black men that they are not bound in some degree by the limits of blackness does not alter the force of the facts.

The National Conference on Black Power was overwhelmingly attended by middle-class-oriented black people. Late, but let us hope not too late, black men are learning that their fortunes are tied together. Ironically, the mounting dislocations in our central cities are reminding at least a few white people—whose numbers must quickly increase—that their fortunes, too, and the survival of the entire nation may be tied to what is perceived in each city as the local equivalent of a Central Ward.

2. The West Ward.   Separating the Central Ward from the Vailsburg section of Newark is the community known as the West Ward. It is a kind of suburban Central Ward in that its buildings are slightly less deteriorated and the rents are slightly higher.

In previous years, the area was made up of families of Italian, Irish, and German origin. The exodus of whites from the area has been precipitous. It is described in *Newark: A City in Transition* as "generally a deteriorating community with crowded frame structures and brick tenements."

Unlike the Central Ward, the total population of the West Ward has remained stable. In 1950 the total population was 62,600; in 1960 it had decreased by only 115 to 62,485.

It must be noted here that population figures for predominantly black slum-type communities tend to be inaccurate. They may vary from 5 percent to as high as 15 percent from a realistic count because of the substantial numbers of "faceless" people who prefer to remain anonymous. "Why should I let 'the man' know who and where I am?" asked one such anonymous person in Newark. He added, " 'The man' will only oppress me anyway."

The perceptions of these people are ironically underscored by the language of the federal census itself. In the census, black people are termed "non-white." A negative being is a nobody. Why enlist yourself, it is reasoned, as not being someone you are **not?**

This suggests that, instead of there being a slight reduction in population size in the West Ward, there might have been an actual increase of more than slender proportions. Nonetheless, the statistics as they are tell a story as dramatic as it is true.

According to official statistics as of 1960, the West Ward had the second highest proportion of black people in a still preponderantly white community in Newark. The white population in 1960 was 36,591 while the black population was 25,693. Most of the black people in the West Ward moved into the community between 1950 and 1960. In 1950 only three of the 12 census tracts in the West Ward had more than 1,000 black people. These were tracts 13, 17, and 38. These tracts were comprised of persons having a relatively high income and educational level and a relatively low employment rate for the city as a whole.

Such figures indicate that at least portions of the West Ward during the 1940's had served for the more fortunate as a place of escape from the black heartland in and around the Central Ward of Newark. Map III shows the location of tract 17 on the East Orange line and tract 13 bounded by Bergen Street, South Orange Avenue, 6th and 8th Streets, and 11th and 12th Avenues. It shows tract 38 adjacent to the Clinton Hill district.

Still, the black people of Newark, even when they escaped toward the periphery of the city, moved into areas of the greatest blight. The West Ward in 1960 actually had 6,766 deteriorating dwellings, representing a higher proportion than that of the Central Ward. The Central Ward had more than three times the number of buildings ready for demolition, the figures being 1,372 dilapidated buildings in the West Ward and 4,941 in the Central Ward. The total dwelling unit figures for the West Ward were 19,053 and for the Central Ward 19,369.

⟨The movement into blighted areas in our cities gives promise of families in perpetual motion, as buildings are vacated for purposes of anticipated renewal. Hence, voter registrations and the record of actual voting tend to be low, since sojourners possessed of a tent-dweller outlook are not motivated to take the continual pains either to reregister or to vote. It is a general rule that migrants do not vote.⟨The black Newarker is effectively kept as a continual migrant. So long as this pattern continues—and it promises to remain for some time—black residents of Newark cannot hope to be

MAP III Correspondence Between Tracts with Low Family Income and Those with Low Educational Attainment, April 1960

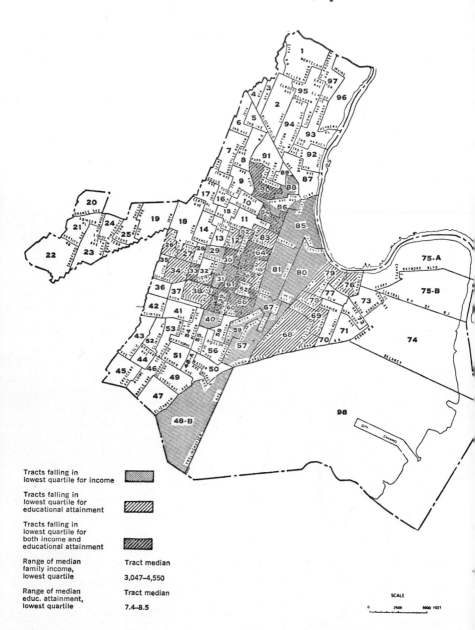

Tracts falling in
lowest quartile for income

Tracts falling in
lowest quartile for
educational attainment

Tracts falling in
lowest quartile for
both income and
educational attainment

Range of median family income, lowest quartile	Tract median 3,047–4,550
Range of median educ. attainment, lowest quartile	Tract median 7.4–8.5

SCALE

0   2500   5000 FEET

SOURCE: U.S. Department of Labor, Bureau of Labor Statistics.

efficiently productive in promoting civic change or in controlling their own destiny by means of the ballot box.

Thus the West Ward promises to extend the frustrations experienced by black people in the Central Ward in terms of the relative powerlessness that is the parent of hopelessness and despair. Unkempt neighborhoods, rising welfare client lists, high dropout and failure rates in the schools, self-hate, and the sense that life means no more than survival are the inevitable products of the current dynamics of such population change. The West Ward is adjacent to Vailsburg. Those who have sought to be most secure share both directly and indirectly in the building of a tinder box next door.）

3. Clinton Hill. Clinton Hill is situated immediately to the south of the West and Central Wards and separates an area of relatively long-time black concentration from the attractive and predominately Jewish community of Weequahic. Several of the finest synagogue structures in Essex County are located there.

Clinton Hill has the highest proportion of home ownership of any predominantly black community in the city. Out of 12,936 dwelling units in the area, 2,673 are owner-occupied. The area also has the city's fourth highest number of deteriorating buildings. Hence, the precipitous rush of black people into the area promises to become but another chapter in the ever-saddening story of musical chairs.

Every important city in the nation reflects in some degree this same pattern of long-term removal of black people into areas that hold the promise of decay. No sooner settled than anticipation of another move becomes tomorrow's reality. Moving after settling down can be a clearly "unsettling" experience. For those who are moved about continuously an unsettled spirit may become their way of life. This works against the development of community pride and the sense of civic investment that provide the foundation for equity and orderly progress in the ongoing life of our cities.

The three census tracts in Clinton Hill that experienced the most dramatic changeover from white to black between 1950 and 1960 are tracts 40, 55, and 56. Tract 40 contained 3,301 white people in 1950, but by 1960 this figure had decreased to 835. Tract 56 experienced a decrease in white population from 3,116 in 1950

MAP IV Correspondence Between Tracts with Low Family Income and Those with High Unemployment, April 1960

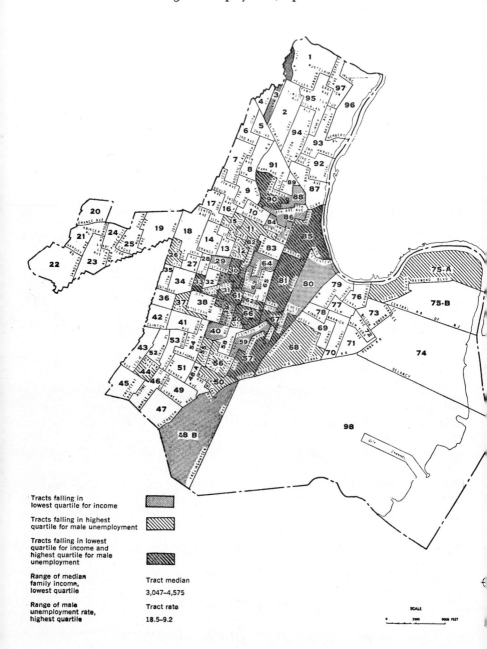

Tracts falling in lowest quartile for income

Tracts falling in highest quartile for male unemployment

Tracts falling in lowest quartile for income and highest quartile for male unemployment

Range of median family income, lowest quartile

Tract median
3,047–4,575

Range of male unemployment rate, highest quartile

Tract rate
18.5–9.2

SCALE

SOURCE: U.S. Department of Labor, Bureau of Labor Statistics.

to 668 in 1960. These three tracts are in the lower Clinton Hill area, at the end farthest from the suburban overwhelmingly white city of Irvington. They represent the area's lowest family incomes and its highest male unemployment rates. This is evident on Map IV.

The rapid changeover from white to black is evidenced by the black population increase during the decade 1950–60 in three more of the community's nine census tract areas. Area 41 moved from 28 to 2,719. Area 54 moved from 229 to 4,251. Area 58 moved from 514 to 3,575.

The remaining three census tract areas—42, 52, and 53—in Clinton Hill have continued to be predominantly white. Map IV shows the location of these areas to be adjacent or near Weequahic on one side and adjacent to Irvington on another. In 1960 the area was 42.74 percent white and 56.98 percent black.

The black population became a majority in Clinton Hill during the same period in which the overall population increased from 33,400 in 1950 to 41,289 in 1960. Since a negligible number of new housing units were made available in the area, this reflects the tragic tendency to overcrowd or to subdivide existing living quarters. Rents in Clinton Hill are next to the highest in the city. At an average of $78.00 monthly as of 1960, they are equal to those in Vailsburg and are exceeded only by the rents in Weequahic that average $84.00 monthly by the 1960 accounting.

The Clinton Hills of our cities provide us with the opportunity both to repay a debt and again, and far more important, to help save ourselves from headlong self-destruction. Black people should own homes, not rent them.

It costs less overall for the federal government to subsidize home ownership than it does to subsidize rents. Apart from the important aspect of basic economy, renters tend to add to social costs from a lack of both civic investment and community pride. Our democratic way of life is based largely upon the recognition that freeholders, those who own property, will take a longer range view of both local and national interest. Renters tend to be relatively less responsible. Our government subsidy programs have locked black people, generally, into the status of renters. As a result, we effectively subsidize renter-related irresponsibilty and

TABLE VIII   Owner-Renter Occupied Dwellings by Community, Newark, 1960

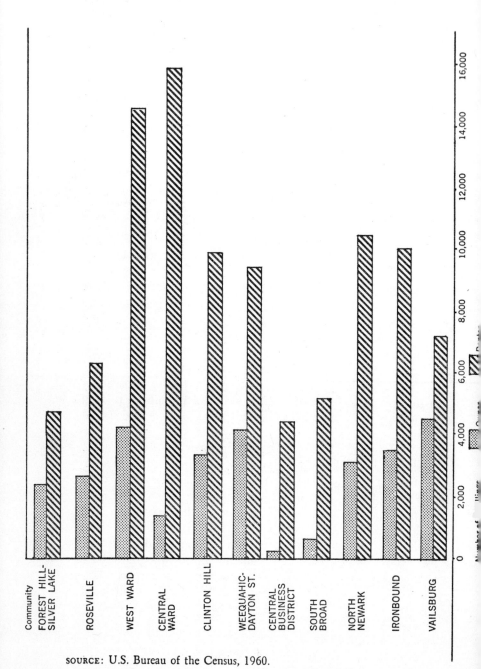

parasitism among the black people of our cities. Table VIII reflects the high disproportion of renters in the predominantly black communities of Newark. Home ownership, even for the white communities, should be increased in all of our cities. The federal government, which has encouraged the present rentership pattern, should take the lead in discouraging further rentership and in encouraging or mandating far greater home ownership, especially for our black urban population.

The Federal Housing Administration (FHA), by insuring low-interest loans to the public at the tax payers' expense, blocked black people from equitable opportunity to share in federally subsidized home purchasing. In 1938 the official FHA *Underwriting Manual* warned home-buyers: "If a neighborhood is to retain stability, it is necessary that properties shall continue to be occupied by the same social and racial group." Restrictive covenants were recommended to keep out "inharmonious racial groups." Further, the FHA urged its mortagage evaluators to ascertain whether "effective restrictive covenants against the entire tract are recorded, since these provide the surest protection against undesirable encroachment . . ." History has shown to the FHA and to others that these policies have helped undermine our cities.

Black people have been locked out of home ownership, which has been most readily available in the suburbs. Homeowners protect property; they do not destroy it. Nonetheless, the damaging effects of this former FHA policy have not been compensated for. Indeed, such policies may be seen to be a part of the continuing pattern of repression.

I shall never forget my first experience of seeing our home from an airplane. Stretched out before us was a tremendous view of the landscape extending for many miles. In a wide perspective, I could see and sense something more of my own place as a responsible trustee of the land that is ours to enjoy. Historically in this nation, black people have worked the land but not owned it. They should be encouraged to own the cities, if the cities are to be the places where black men are destined to live. No more low-rent housing should be built for black people. The federal government subsidized the blocking out of black people from home ownership in the past. It must now repay the debt, with at least some portion of the interest due.

4. Central Business District. The Central Business District, or CBD, is the area containing the primary and secondary core of the business life of Newark. Primary businesses involve direct or basic production providing the foundation for the city's economy. Secondary businesses are those created to support the primary functioning enterprises.

The Central Business District of Newark is a major office center. It is the second largest insurance headquarters in the nation. The area presently serves as one of the major centers for Newark's redevelopment activity. The Newark campus of Rutgers—the State University—is a principal part of this redevelopment. Middle-income housing, projected in the early 1960's and begun substantially by 1966, has come to a stand-still as a result of the 1967 civic strife.

Several small but attractive parks grace the Central Business District, and handsome office buildings and old church steeples form a thin line of beauty along a portion of Newark's main thoroughfare, Broad Street. There are a few scattered residential sections in the CBD comprising a population in 1960 of 12,914, up by 414 over the 1950 census figure of 12,500.

Map III shows tracts 80, 81, and 85 as falling into the lowest quatrile for income and the highest quatrile for male unemployment. *Newark: A City in Transition, Vol. III,* reports that 33 percent of the population of the Central Business District in 1958 was Puerto Rican. No official figures are available from the 1960 census, as Puerto Ricans variously list themselves as white, Negro, and Puerto Rican. That Puerto Ricans are received into deteriorating neighborhoods finds support in the statistics for deteriorating housing in the Central Business District where nearly one-half (or 2,307) of the 5,105 dwelling units are reported to be deteriorating. Of the area's residents, 6,153 reported themselves as black. Hence, the CBD may be classified as an area of black succession into population predominance. Table VIII summarizes the white-black population proportions by communities in Newark as of 1960.

The Central Business Districts of America characteristically reflect a pattern of growing black predominance at their edges, white business predominance at the center, a skid row, a cultural center, and either vacated land for anticipated "middle-income" housing or the actuality of some middle- and higher-income apartments, occupied primarily by white people. Newark is no exception. It reflects faulty design from a faulty perception of what are basically the needs of our cities.

People who look as if their horizons have not been widened, who show no evidence that their sense of dignity and self-awareness has been quickened. Such is the daily sight in the diners and the bars near the Four Corners, at Broad and Market Streets, Newark, at the center of the CBD. Such is the view as one passes the lines of people entering the offices of the public welfare or going into the CBD's easy credit stores along lower Washington Street and up the hill along Springfield Avenue. Newark's new urban extension of Rutgers, the State University, in the CBD does not speak basically to the needs of these people. Rutgers graciously offers special courses and special inducements to black youth who fall below its normal standards for entry. This is a glorious thing, but admittedly not calculated to rehabilitate the adult urban poor, let alone the growing numbers of those thrust by self-will or by circumstances out of the traditional public education process.

The cultural or acculturation agencies in the nation's Central Business Districts must come to see the new needs that lie ahead. They cannot deal with these needs from the present orientation of our institutions of "higher" learning. Our colleges and universities, unless they are to become increasingly anachronistic, must learn that education is for people, not people for the educational structure or agency "as it was . . . and ever shall be," with major or minor "progressive" improvements here and there.

Rutgers is ostensibly designed to speak to urban needs. The most pressing "urban" needs in Newark are coming to be those of black people in the most desperate immediate terms. How can Rutgers "empower" these black people for fulfillment or help to promote a substantial change in the relations of equity and investment in city life? The efforts of good faith that have been made are a small but far too inadequately conceived beginning.

One basic opportunity for spawning change was missed—and understandably so in the light of our cultural habits—when the new administration of the expanded Newark Rutgers was appointed. The State University, along with every major business enterprise and civic or social agency in the CBD, should have enlisted an equitable number of black men of great potential for top level, decision-making, administrative, and executive leadership offices. With the best potential among black people having gone into education in the past, a rudimentary sense of justice would mean that able black educators should be at the helm of the major urban educational systems in the nation. The fact that this kind of elementary justice has not prevailed for black professionals suggests something of the even larger handicaps that black pupils must labor under *within the schools,* let alone the problems built into their learning potential from outside.

The Central Business Districts of the nation are white-owned, white-controlled, and white purposed. As we shall see graphically in the chapter that follows, our cities cannot create for themselves a balanced life so necessary to orderly progress under such one-sided conditions. That these CBD men of leadership are possessed of aggressive good will is not enough. They must be awakened to new and urgent realities. Some white social scientists and civic, business, and political leaders are seeking valiantly to create such new awarenesses, but the burden cannot be placed upon white people whose perceptions about what are basically black people's needs are developed largely secondhand. Black civic, business, and political leaders, together with the most able black social scientists, must take a new leadership role in terms of clarification, interpretation, and the setting of a new and more enlightened agenda for our cities. The fact that one is black, as a growing myth would have it, does not make a man omnicompetent, but our blackness should make us far more sensitive to the critical relationship between survival and the facing of new and urgent realities.

5. **South Broad Street.** South Broad is a residential appendage to the Central Business District. A few fine old residences still remain in the community, but most are now converted into business uses. Over one-half the buildings in the neighborhood housing some sixteen thousand persons are either deteriorating or dilapidated. The community was reported to be 57.11 percent black in 1960 and 42.58 percent white. The South Broad Streets of our cities, as areas of black population sojourn, promise to be marked by the same vicious cycle of removal and dislocation—with the

attendant personal, social, and civic trauma—as that which characterizes the other portions of the "rotten casket."

Violence to the human spirit, as evidenced by the unconscious unwillingness or inability to let our black newcomers stay still long enough in a neighborhood to sink their roots in civic soil, means aborted life for our cities. The fact that Newark has the largest proportion of land set aside for urban renewal of any major city in the nation suggests in an ominous way the fresh problems that may be in store.

The white-controlled civic and municipal agencies, left with the responsibility for servicing the soaring and erratic needs of the black newcomers in perpetual motion, inevitably have reflected bewilderment. The continuing inability for the white leadership remaining in the city to solve the mounting social and economic problems has led to escapism and entrenchment.

John T. Cunningham wrote of the black people of Newark as having been locked into the heart of the city in the early 1940's. He relates: "Already the suburbs had silently closed their doors to the Negroes. Each day during the war busloads of Negro workers had rolled westward out of Newark, travelling forty to fifty miles one way to the Morris County powder plants. It would have made more sense for them to live near their jobs, *but suburban communities closed ranks against non-white residents.*" (Italics mine.)[6]

Aggressive suppression of black people in Newark began at least a quarter of a century ago. The same pattern in many forms has been experienced by black men over the years. In the next chapter it will be seen as a basis for or a manifestation of the generalized condition of hostility, consternation, and rampage, among white and black urbanites alike, that we refer to as riot or civic rebellion.

[6] *Newark*, pp. 299–300.

3 Unplanned Exploitation: Social Costs

The mounting problems and diminishing resources faced by the City of Newark during the twenty-year period following World War II were representative of an unplanned but growing condition throughout the nation.

METROPOLITAN GROWTH

National trends pointed to what city planners called a process of metropolitan growth. Population was spreading out from the cities. Small communities nearby were no longer removed from the urban scene, as the people who left swelled the numbers of those living in the once-remote suburban towns and occupied the open spaces that formerly buffered these towns from the city.

The process, however unplanned, appeared reasonable. The American dream of a plot of land and a single family home exercised an inevitable pull on those who were influenced by the idealism of the war and were weary of being subjected to the crippling inconveniences of sustained wartime urban life.

City life also had its fresh deficiencies. Taxes were rising, with no end to the spiral in sight. New people with new problems were entering in large numbers. The demand for city services—in terms of health, education, welfare, transportation, police and fire protection, physical rehabilitation, and other aspects of social, economic, and political concern—staggered the imagination of those who understood the workings of the city.

On the surface it was far simpler, and immediately less costly, to leave the central city than to remain under circumstances as they were and were about to be. Hundreds of thousands accepted the option to leave. Their departure for the suburban cities and towns deprived the central city of much of its traditional and more experienced leadership. The decrease in economic returns from the skills of these more highly trained people left the central city with the effects of mass departure. Indeed, the control of and economic benefits from the central city's institutional life were taken away to an even greater degree than in the past.

Aggravating the growing deficit of resources even further was the postwar abandonment by industry, leaving fewer employment opportunites nearby for the lower skilled and the unskilled who remained in or came into the city. Stripped of much of its leadership and other resources, and faced with problems from before and after the war, the city came to be like a house ransacked.

But these represented only the readily observable symptoms of destitution. From time immemorial the city has served the suburbs as a place of exploitation *par excellence.* A man born blind in the suburbs will tend to spend his adult life and declining years in the city, where there are fewer walking patterns to memorize for basic needs. In the city there is a greater concentration of health and welfare services to assist those who need—and cannot afford while living elsewhere—the care of others.

The suburbs and the more remote towns and villages of America tend to have as their inhabitants highly motivated, hard-working, healthy, highly intelligent, and self-directed people. This is so because the subnormal, the diseased, the disabled, and those who cannot or who have not been allowed to fit into their patterns of life have gone or been sent to the city. Basically problems do not grow up in urban life. They are poured in, almost unconsciously, as though this process was ordained by eternal arrangement. This is done with apparent good intent, for those with personal problems and with diseased or disordered lives find services in the city that provide temporary relief for their pain and a kind of saving or at least sedating anonymity. Problems are—and through the ages have been—thrust upon the city from without. Life has been kept pleasant in the suburbs at urban expense, in terms of the downgrading of the total environment of the central city. The recent mass exodus to the suburbs simply added to prevaling inequities.

Nor is the nation as a whole to escape blameless in the city's plight. It is the nation as a whole that decides immigration policies. The major cities receive the immigrants and must service the initial adjustment and continuing needs of the immigrants. The concentration of newcomers in the process of accommodation to the nation's ways creates fresh civic, political, and economic burdens. It also conditions the environment of those who grow up in the city by a weighting toward low educational attainment, low economic level, and a proportionately high level of dependency of various kinds. The role models of the city tend to limit levels of aspiration by comparison with such models for those who grow up in suburbia.

Economic conditions have influenced migration from the farms to the city. National farm policy has had its added effects. Likewise, regional social and economic conditions, especially in the rural South, have determined the trek of black people principally into the central cities of the nation's northeast and far west.

Can the cities halt the migrants at the door as they seek to enter, inevitably to add fresh burdens? The suburbs tend to do so. And suburbanites own the properties into which the migrants are crowded and then kept. Suburbanites reap the immediate economic benefits from human misery in the city. Suburbanites use the cities' services and help concentrate urban problems.

The nation as a whole takes largely the same "suburbanite" view of the city. The cities are seen to exist for the convenience of the nation, to be exploited for the all-too-easy benefit of one and all. But this thoughtless, myopic attitude has been chiefly responsible for bringing us close to the day of disaster.

Unplanned metropolitan growth after World War II—with its precipitous increase of a long-standing suburban and national exploitation of the cities—has been the primary catalyst of our mounting urban distress.

This pattern may be illustrated by focusing upon the recent life of Newark. Between 1950 and 1960 the City of Newark lost 8 percent of its population, while its county, Essex, gained overall by 2 percent. Between 1950 and 1960, 8 percent of Newark's dwelling units were erected, chiefly through urban renewal and in the form of public housing; 26 percent of the dwelling units in the county as a whole were built during the same decade. These figures indicate that substantial numbers of people had left the city and had moved into the immediate and more remote suburbs, where there was newer housing and presumably more space.

But these people continued to work in the city. A quarter of a million people enter Newark each day as a part of the movement of people and goods. Approximately one-half of Newark's two hundred thousand jobs are filled by people who live in the suburbs. Newark has the greatest proportionate daytime population turnover of any major city in the country. It is a tribute to those who direct the traffic that the day migrants are ushered in and out. It is also indicative of the increased burdens placed upon the city for such services as road building and maintenance, for police and fire protection, and for water supply. Police requirements alone are so great by day that Newark admits it cannot afford adequate protection for its full time residents by night.

Whenever a city has a high daytime population turnover, this is symptomatic of exploitation. For nowhere in America—except in a few county-municipal governments—have barely reasonable approaches even begun to be made to treat the cities as more than wells to be drained or as refuse heaps on which to discard the problems of suburbia and of the entire nation. Clearly needed planning for equity and investment in total metropolitan life has not even been attempted for the needy newcomers to the city; nor has this been done for the city as a whole. Our best planning in the past and present has been geared to the view that cities are the physical environment in which people live, largely within narrowly defined local political limits.

BLACK LEADERSHIP EXODUS

During the decade between 1950 and 1960, the black population of Essex County increased by approximately 75,000, with 63,000 of this number being added to the City of Newark. Even here, the bulk of the 12,000 black population increase for the county outside of Newark was represented by people moving from Newark. These suburban-bound black people were primarily the more highly trained and affluent who could not gain access to dwelling units in the Forest Hill, Vailsburg, or Weequahic communities.

The U.S. Bureau of Labor Statistics Report No. 332, "Social and Economic Conditions of Negroes in the United States," dated October, 1967, states: "As Negro families succeed, they tend to move out of . . . economically and socially depressed areas to better neighborhoods where they and their children have the opportunity to lead a better life. They leave behind increasing problems of deprivation in the heart of our largest cities." (Page XII.) The departure of middle-class black people from Newark, and from central cities across the nation, has represented a hazardous drain upon a resource crucial for the new civic, political, and economic adjustments the cities have had to face.

The greatest unused trained leadership potential in our metropolitan areas has been and is the much maligned so-called black middle class. These are people whose roots are in the city; and more than for any other potential leadership group, their economic fortunes and civic status and security are tied up with the fortunes of the distraught, black urban masses. But uniquely in our history of rising ethnic groups, black people, especially in our northern cities, have been deprived of much of the sense of group solidarity that would have enabled them—as have other such groups—to contribute most substantially to the power dynamics of city life.

At the very time that group pride and solidarity for black people was most urgently needed, the historical accident of what was in part at least a faultily conceived but well-intentioned emphasis upon integration in various forms took hold. It had the unanticipated side effect of diminishing the group influence of trained black people and of inadvertently adding to the prevailing black lack of identity and the black group sense of self-hate. This has manifested itself in the recent skyrocketing of social, civic, and criminal patterns of self-destruction within the black community. The open warfare in our city streets is, in part at least, expressive of self-hate. It is black suicide in the presence of white men's bullets.

A picture of the type of black person moving into the suburbs largely from Newark is suggested by patterns of black population change in the nearby suburban municipalities of East Orange and Montclair. The black population in East Orange moved from 7 percent in 1940 to 11 percent in 1950. In 1960, 25 percent of the population of East Orange was black, and in 1966 East Orange's specifically black population was estimated to be as high as 37 percent. By 1970, even with extensive relocation because of expressway construction, it is projected that approximately 40 percent of the population of East Orange will be black. In Montclair, the change has been more gradual than in East Orange. The black population as of 1940 was 18 percent, in 1950 it was 20 percent, in 1960 it was 23 percent, and in 1965 it was estimated to be 26 percent.

East Orange and Montclair are among the more affluent areas of Greater Newark. The average family income in 1960 for East Orange was $5,631 and for Montclair it was $6,494. In the predominantly black census tract areas, which also represent those of the lowest family incomes in East Orange and Montclair, the 1960 average family incomes were $4,945.80 for East Orange and $4,516.82 for Montclair. The figures suggest that in East Orange the increased black population is more nearly representative of the community as a whole economically than is the case with Montclair. Similarly, in 1960 the median years of schooling in these lowest income black areas of East Orange and Montclair were 10.93 and 10.26 respectively. The median years of schooling for these communities as a whole are 11.5 for East Orange and 12.4 for Montclair.

Clearly the untutored migrant newcomers were not making their mass entry into these suburban communities that experienced the bulk of the county's suburban black population increase. The median family income of Newark's black population in 1960 was $4,000. The average number of school years completed by the Newark population was nine years. This was considerably less than that of the predominantly black sections of East Orange and Montclair.

The entire City of Newark needed the leadership potential of these more highly trained black people who were settling in East Orange and Montclair. The black newcomers needed the relationship of the so-called black middle class in the most urgent way. Yet the period between 1950 and 1965 saw a diminishing of the in-group influence of trained black people, as "integration" came to be like a magic rainbow at the end of which was the pot containing the supposed cure-all for black people's ills.

I remember all too well the social routine forced upon so many black people during this largely abortive period in the social development of the nation. Whenever we were to be a part of a group of white and black people, we would make certain that we as black people did not congregate as a group. Indeed, things went so far that black people often would not speak to each other in the presence of whites. Sometimes this is still the case. So-called integration became in part a form of self-deprecation.

While other rising ethnic groups built power blocs that gave them a voice in the determination of civic, political, and economic affairs, black men and women possessed of the greatest leadership possibilities followed the path of flight to the suburbs. Black people outdid white people in trying to be white. The black communities in Newark—and in all our major cities—have been fragmented in such a way that self-development became impossible when the impetus toward self-sufficiency was needed most. Minority group self-hate is often worse than oppression from without.

Table IX indicates for the early 1960's the results of what was even then the national trend toward lack of ethnic group solidarity among black people. People who do not control their own destinies are controlled from without. The failure or incapacity to control one's own destiny always opens the way to exploitation. It is responsible for a culture of mounting dependency.

The results of a lack of ethnic group solidarity and purpose are clearly evident in Table IX. In 1961 Detroit, for example, had only slightly more than one-third of the proportionate city council membership that should have come from its hard-pressed black

TABLE IX Negro Representation on City Councils in Selected Non-Southern Cities, 1961[1]

CITY	TOTAL CITY COUNCIL SEATS	SEATS HELD BY NEGROES IN 1961	PERCENT OF SEATS HELD BY NEGROES	NEGROES AS PERCENT OF POPULATION, 1960
Detroit	9	1	11.1	28.9
Cleveland	33	8	24.2	28.6
St. Louis	29	6	20.7	28.6
Philadelphia	17	1	5.9	26.4
Chicago	50	6	12.0	22.9
Cincinnati	9	0	0	21.6
New York City	25	2	8.0	14.0
Los Angeles	15	0	0	13.5
Boston	9	0	0	9.1
Newark	9	1	11.1	35.0

[1] This Table is a revised version (to include Newark) of the one given by Edward Banfield and James Q. Wilson in *City Politics* (Cambridge, Mass.: Harvard-MIT Press, 1963), p. 293. Adapted by Sharon Perlman, Douglass College.

community. It is the black people who are destined to be the longest-term residents or wards of the city. Their long-range self-interest should square best with the long-range interests of the city.

Of the ten major cities compared, Cleveland came closest to its duly proportionate black representation. In 1967 it elected its first black mayor.

There may be some correlation between the size of city councils and the proportion of black representation. St. Louis, with a large number of council seats, had nearly two-thirds of its proportionate black representation. Chicago and New York City, also with large councils, had more than half their proportionate black representation according to black population size.

On the other hand, those selected major cities with small city councils (under 20 members), showed the smallest proportionate number of black city councilmen. Philadelphia, with 17 seats, had one black councilman in 1961, while black people represented more than 26 percent of the population. Los Angeles, with 15 councilmen and over 13 percent black population proportion, had no black councilmen in 1961. Nor did Boston or Cincinnati, both with 9 councilmen and a 9 percent and 21 percent black population proportion respectively, have any black councilmen as of 1961. Newark, with 9 councilmen and a 35 percent black population proportion, had 1 councilman, or one-third of its proportion in relation to the population as a whole. These figures suggest several factors directly related to the unplanned exploitation of the city.

UNSHARED POWER

Those who have held the reigns of power in our cities have not aggressively facilitated the political empowerment of the weak. Only where council seats were numerous enough, according to the statistics in Table IX, were black people given most nearly equitable council representation. Large councils, then, would seem to serve at least the temporary advantage of numerically equitable representation by black people.

That those in power would not tend to facilitate equitable representation for black people is understandable when note is taken of the kind of people with power who reside in the cities. They are the people who have entrenched themselves in the communities typified by the Vailsburgs, Forest Hills, Rosevilles, Weequahics, Ironbounds, and North Wards. These people, if not anti-black, would certainly not tend to be pro-black.

People who are placed in the position of taking a last ditch stand against change that is clearly associated with mounting costs, diminishing resources, and galloping blight would not welcome with open arms a stranger whose presence seemed to bring with it the plague. This was something akin to the perceptions of white people left behind by those whites who fled the city; they began to feel pressed by the outward movement of newcomers whose presence changed old relationships and made the City of Newark seem like a strange and eerie land.

White people with the reins of power have seen their cities swept by blight. The fact that black newcomers took shelter in homes that had progressively deteriorated since the beginning of the Great Depression had little impact upon those white people who were left on the edges of the city. The ready perception for all to quickly see was the coming, in time, of black people along with the signs of gross decay. The fact that urban renewal, with its "black removal," has been a major catalyst in the spread of massive property depreciation was also of small significance to those caught up in a condition of apparent impossibilities at every hand.

Federal funds were available for land clearance. The cities seemed to have had no other choice but to clear large tracts of land. Even the growing blight and later the land clearance served unwittingly the interests of exploitation. For a time at least, large profits were made by those who had left the city and who could rent subdivided and substandard properties to black people at far higher rents than were paid by former white tenants. In Boston where I served for fourteen years as a parish clergyman, our rectory —originally in an overwhelmingly white neighborhood—suddenly came to be surrounded by black people. This came about as the result of urban renewal land clearance in Boston's predominantly black South End. Apartment buildings near our rectory had been occupied principally by older white people paying modest rents and with an average of 1.5 persons in each dwelling unit. With urban renewal, the property became occupied by black people. Subdividing occurred. Rents trebled, and family size, even in smaller units, was more than doubled. This is the sad and universal story of the Roxburys, the Clinton Hills, the West Wards, and the other areas that mark the first step toward advancing slums in every major city of the land.

In the early 1960's, federal housing officials, whose bureaucratic history had been marked only recently by commitment to some semblance of fair play for black people by eliminating restrictive criteria, were no major aggressive resource in posing thoughtful approaches to the political needs of black people caught up in the spread of housing decay. So long as black people were on the move, however, neither black political consciousness nor black community and group pride could grow. Unintended circumstances associated with urban renewal thus have had their adverse effect upon the morale of black communities, and hence the cities themselves.

"Only a staff of full-time clerks and organizers could have kept up with those who were changing their addresses on the voting lists in the Central Ward," reports Eulice Ward, Democratic Chairman of Newark's predominantly black Central Ward. Ward added, "Urban renewal has meant political death for black people in Newark. With the medical-dental school coming, new roadways and the other land clearances already planned, Newark's black folks are in for many long, hot summers. We haven't a ghost of a chance to develop real political power."

This is a bad omen for the city. The prevailing powerlessness of black people in the central cities of the nation has bred despair and self-hate. It has enabled those already frustrated by mounting lists of insolvable city problems to govern badly and with impunity. Hence inadequate schools, poor police practices, ineffective building and sanitary code enforcement, coercive penal and welfare services, and perpetual problems in a host of other politically related areas are all a part of the accepted way of life in Newark and in the urban black heartlands across the country. Those who can govern unchallenged may govern with contempt.

Such has been the case with regard to black people without equitable political power in our cities. Such also is the case with others who find that they are possessed of even less political power in many of our cities. The remnant of the formerly powerful white Anglo-Saxon Protestant community in Newark, and elsewhere, finds that its capacity to influence civic decisions has been swept away. This was made crystal clear in 1966 when a group of white Protestant clergy approached the Mayor of Newark regarding conditions in the schools. "But you represent no voting strength!" was the Mayor's telling response. The sad but understandable counterresponse has been for the white Protestants in Newark to become escapist. They tend to ignore civic issues, to define issues in escapist ways, or one by one to make their shamefaced exits to the suburbs.

The white Protestant communities in our cities have preached what they have believed to be liberalism. They have initiated grand projects for relating to black people, but have done so as white people and as white institutions. Hence, white churches with white leadership, and with resources to remain white and survive, have remained under white leadership and control. There has been no sustained and widespread effort in any major city for white churches to encourage black pastoral leadership—and hence a change in power and status relations—except in areas of actual or anticipated racial transition. "The white churches, with the greatest goodwill, have missed the point of redemption," says Detroit's black militant pastor, the Reverend Albert Cleage; "Mankind cries out at this perilous hour for freedom, and not for flexibility within its chains."

A leader of the Episcopal Diocese of Newark explains in a sympathetic way what the churches have done. He writes:

As we have sought to do the Great Physician's work in the city over the past 20 years and more, no one can doubt that the churches of all faiths have shown exemplary care and concern. The goodwill and earnest intention of the churches to ameliorate the needs of those who live in the city have been expressed in unprecedented financial commitments to new urban exploratory programs. The Diocese of Newark has been a leader in this regard.

We have now come to realize, however, that the work of the Great Physician is done not only in the sick room but also at the operating table. If redemption is to be brought to the total life of the city, the Great Physician must also serve as Surgeon. In this regard, our churches must now greatly expand the horizons of our concern.

However, the past emphasis of the churches has been to do all that was necessary to preserve the usefulness of their property and the integrity of their unconsciously white-purposed concerns. The precipitous changes that have come upon our cities have taken every institution in our society, in large measure, unaware. The immediate instinct in the face of unexpected new developments is to hold on for dear life to what is being swept away. That this has led the churches into the prevailing pattern of unplanned exploitation of the city must be seen as incidental to a clear and wholly positive spirit. The churches, along with other institutions, can and must shift their operations to correspond with new insights.

Throughout the nation, the white Protestant community, which could have meant much to urban peace and progress, has fled or lived largely oblivious to the basic needs of those who live in the city. This community has controlled and still controls much of our cities' economic life. The way is now open as never before for its members to vindicate themselves and to help save the nation in its present plight.

INTERPRETING URBAN NEEDS

The break-up of ethnic group populations, and their separation from their native trained leadership potential, may be a liability for our cities. This seems to be implicit in an assessment of the 1961 city council representation by black people in the ten selected cities in Table IX.

Certainly in Newark this has served to fracture the political power of black people. It has aggravated the effects of the well-nigh universal pattern in our cities to gerrymander black voting districts. The use of the gerrymander device is a repressive tactic. It is a reflection of the long-standing pattern of violence against black people in our cities by those who hold political power.

Black men and women of training who have left our cities represent an almost incalculable loss politically. That high taxes and increasing inconveniences have impelled them to leave the city is as understandable as it is unfortunate. It is also readily understandable how things came to be as they are. Yet our understanding alone, without forthright and aggressive commitment to thoughtful change, will not save our cities from peril.

Until all people in our cities have a sense that they have worth as persons, until they are educated toward the realization of their very best capacities, the cities cannot possibly avoid continuing unrest. This is in the self-interest of the nation. It is in the safety and survival interests of our suburbs. It is most immediately related to the needs of black suburbanites; for the security and the possibilities of civic and economic progress for all black people are directly related to the status of black people *as a whole.*

Howard Thurman is said to have told a parable of the turtle that illustrates extremely well the role educated black men must come to play in our cities. The parable explains that a turtle moves from one place to another or makes "progress" by first extending his head from its shell. Much of the thoughtful reassessment required by our cities must come from black initiative. More than any other single weapon in their fight for freedom—which involves the regeneration of their urban place of residence—black men must employ the monumental resource of their minds. The parable explains that the turtle then pushes his front feet forward. But the turtle can only move toward its destination when its hind legs are put to work, and head and "all fours" function in an interrelated and coordinated fashion. In this way alone, with all resources "pulling together," may black men make the kind of progress that spells well-being for all.

We may see something of the crucial and specific utility of thoughtful black leadership potential as we note several examples of unplanned but gross exploitation of the city effected by the suburbs and the nation.

The population exodus from the cities has been marked by the departure of skills and high incomes and by the entry into the central cities of lower skills, lower educational attainment, smaller income potential, and a higher incidence of dependency. Welfare costs have mounted and the total environment for nurture and growth has become depressed.

Our urban centers attract overall a highly disproportionate number of persons in need of community resources. The taxpayer left behind in the city must pay to bear increased direct and indirect burdens created by the presence of large numbers of undereducated people with a low aspiration level. Even where county, state, and national resources pay for certain welfare costs, the cities must also pay many direct costs for the maintenance of those who need relief. The concentration of problem people in Newark is typified by the state aid to dependent children statistics. The City of Newark represents approximately 7 percent of the population of the state of New Jersey but accounts for more than 35 percent of the state aid to dependent children costs. This means, at the outset, that at least five times the average amount of this category of family relief commitments for the communities of the state is spent in the City of Newark.

Problem concentration of one kind calls for the provision of many associated services. Disorganized families mean greater truancy, higher dropout and higher delinquency rates. The residents of the city must pay the costs involved. When these problems are associated primarily with one ethnic group, as they are in Newark and other major cities, the group as a whole is categorized. That ethnic group shares a common relative stigma and relative rejection in the life of our cities. No urban black man, woman, or child can escape fully from the penalty of being part of a group whose needs represent a disproportionately high tax burden upon the public.

Black professionals, especially those who are trained in the social sciences, must both understand for themselves and interpret for others the self-defeating patterns by which there has been an unplanned exploitation of the taxpayers who are left behind in our cities. So long as localism is the rule, unplanned exploitation will occur. For the present, the exploited are in our central cities, their taxpayers and their black citizens locked into limitations at every hand. Next it will be the nearer suburbs, as present signs suggest. Is this the way for a mature and responsible people to provide for their ordered and unfolding life as one nation?

The elderly, with their particular complex of needs, are also concentrated in the cities. Even where remote suburban housing developments are built for them, less self-directed elderly persons and those with the least resources and the greatest problems still tend to be concentrated in our cities. Approximately 20 percent of the state of New Jersey's old age assistance recipients are residents of the City of Newark. A high proportion of people on relief of any kind, however, has a conditioning effect upon the local environment. It affects adults, but more especially it affects children, who later will be either assets or burdens on the entire country. Those who live in or who are brought up in our present urban environment are surrounded by an overabundance of ready images of dependency. Philip Hauser speaks of this environment as determining the "pre-conception I.Q." of children born in the central city. Of the limitations placed upon human development by the unplanned exploitation of our urban environment, Dr. Hauser writes:

The child with a very high pre-conception I.Q. bright enough to select white-skinned parents who live in the suburbs by that astute act, has guaranteed unto himself an input for public primary and secondary school education two to ten times as great as the child with a very low-preconception I.Q. who selects dark-skinned parents who live in an inner-city ghetto. To complete the continuum, the child with an intermediate pre-conception I.Q. bright enough to select white-skinned parents but not bright enough to select residents of a suburb gets an intermediate educational input. That is, the white child in the suburbs gets a first class education, the white child in the city gets a second class education, and the Negro child and the white child in the inner city get a third or fourth rate education. And this in a society that describes itself as a democracy with equality of opportunity![1]

The nation must pay for stunted lives. We may exercise the wanton luxury of failing to anticipate and of failing to plan for the orderly, interrelated, and interdependent life of cities and suburbs, states and nation. By this choice we simply build even further into our cities the condition of continuous riot in terms of white repression, hostility, and exploitative violence to human life on the one hand and black rebellion and the crazed overt destruction of property on the other. Since overt expressions of civic rebellion on the part of black people have the most immediately adverse effects upon the black community as a whole, the self-interest of black leadership is best served when black leaders insist that new devices for systematic, continuous, and comprehensive metropolitan planning are created and utilized.

The City of Newark has led the nation in primary and secondary syphilis case rates and in gonorrhea rates among major American cities. Newark, with its relatively high proportion of dislocated black people, represents what other cities may soon expect. The high incidence of social diseases is related to civic despair. Sexual promiscuity—while widespread—tends to be increased where people feel that they are dehumanized and sense that they have no hope. Its damaging effects can now be felt in contiguous suburban areas.

The growing signs of promiscuity at all levels of our society suggest a clue to our approach to the needs of those who are exploited. Our attitudes toward the least powerful in any situation, whether in our families, our businesses, or our communities, basically reflect our regard, or lack of it, for human life. So the needs of those most greatly exploited are representative of pervasive needs

[1] *Renewal*, December, 1967.

in our society. By addressing ourselves realistically to the needs of the most greatly deprived, we develop handles for dealing with the harder-to-grasp problems in our own life and that of others.

Instruments for relating representative thought from all segments of the black community must be created so that black needs in our cities may be seen as a whole. In no major American city has this been done. It is being attempted presently in New Haven, Connecticut. Groundwork has been laid for some time in Newark, but the absence of professional leadership and staff resources has severely limited the Newark endeavor. The background of the limited experiences in New Haven and Newark should be instructive as we assess the relationship of black leadership to the unplanned exploitation of the cities.

PLANNING FOR BLACK COMMUNITY NEEDS

New Haven has been prominently billed as a model city for the nation. It has had a relatively long and extensive experience of physical rehabilitation. Initiative for planning for the removal of largely black community blight was taken by the white community. It has involved much of the black community at every stage of its unfolding. But the planning and implementation have been persistently white led. Black leaders in New Haven indicate that they doubt that white people in any of our cities have been as kind to black people as have the white people of New Haven, but throughout New Haven's redevelopment, economic returns, policy determination, and management responsibilities have been kept primarily in the hands of white people. In spite of extensive clearance and rebuilding, black people have not developed a sense of power to control their own destinies. Indeed, the physical redevelopment of the city served in a wholly unintended way to further the black sense of exploitation.

In the fall of 1967 I was asked to meet with representatives of the Heritage Hall Committee of the Dixwell Community House, New Haven's only black social settlement. The purpose of the meeting was to explore the possibility of forming a continuing coalition of the broadest possible spectrum of black leadership in New Haven County. The group was led by Henry Parker, a school teacher in one of the suburban towns. Expediter for the meeting was Alfonso Tindall, Executive Director of Dixwell House. Significantly, the steering committee included the local black Episcopal rector, the Muslim minister, the president of the New Haven branch of the National Association for the Advancement of Colored People, an antipoverty official, a young civic leader branded by the press as a militant and who had been arrested during a demonstration for disturbing the peace, a lawyer who served as the public prosecutor for the arrested militant, and the leader of what is held to be the most angry black protest group in the city. The unlikely group met with the idea of engaging my services as its continuing consultant.

Several instructive things were immediately apparent. The steering committee members, and presumably those they represented, expressed a need for the black community's problems to be seen as a whole, no matter how difficult the creation of an operational harmony on the part of representatives of all black groups in New Haven might be. In every city of the nation black people are dealt with in ways that are fragmenting. Neighborhood organization as such has recently accelerated a culturally conditioned tendency toward divisiveness among black people. White government officials and social agency personnel—under the blind mystique of often ill-defined integration—by and large have been unwilling to deal with black people by themselves, despite their peculiarly singular needs.

The steering committee members also felt that a major part of their endeavor should be to create a community leadership task force exclusively made up of white decision-makers with whom the black coalition could deal in effective power-related ways. In addition, they indicated that whatever had failed to come to pass for the benefit of the black community was fundamentally not due to the intentions of the white leadership of New Haven. Rather it was due to the local—as well as historical—failure of black people to devise ways of seeing their problems whole and of developing some semblance of group power.

It is to the credit of the black people of New Haven that this elementary and yet relatively bold effort is being made. It is a credit also to the white citizens of New Haven that so much of the traditional white leadership of that city has been willing to engage in an ongoing response to an agenda for black needs—and so for basic urban human rebuilding—set by representatives of the whole black community. Problems have been encountered in New Haven, and will continue to appear; many of them will be far more difficult than those approached in the past. Yet the solution of problems properly and honestly faced will always lead to some good end.

Here in Newark a similar enterprise at black coalition has been underway for approximately a year and a half. Representatives of a wide range of civil rights organizations have been working in some semblance of operational harmony. They have sought to build a broad coalition but have been faced with difficulties from within and without.

Leaders of the black coalition for Newark learned early in their experience that the needs of Newark's black people could not be met unless black leadership and support from throughout Essex County was utilized for their benefit. Even more important, there was the recognition that in order to deal effectively with the city and county government, sufficient black numerical strength had to be developed to be able to influence the state government at Trenton. The logical form of organization was a network of groups working in operational harmony for political, civic, and economic power in Greater Newark (Essex County), Greater Paterson (Passaic County), and Greater Jersey City (Hudson County). Such a form of organization, later named The Tri-City Community Organization for Development, would be to the advantage of Paterson and Jersey City where the absence of a relatively affluent black community would work against future self-support possibilities. This is not the case in Essex County, but Essex County especially would be required to add to the numerical strength of black people in other areas and to give power to their endeavors.

Leaders of the Tri-City Community Organization for Development during 1967 were caught up in two concerns. The Newark leadership for the group found itself on the verge of what emerged as an open rebellion and civic massacre. Then the group had looked for quick initial funding from an interdenominational body represented by church executives. The church officials had indicated their openness to funding possibilities and had expressed their determination to aid the black community in a substantial and cooperative way.

Preoccupation with pressing immediate situations, rather than with issues relating to the prevailing conditions of black debilitation, has had its crippling effect upon the progress of the tri-city coalition. The group's leaders report a sense of extended frustration at what they have perceived to be an inexcusable slowness to respond to their proposals on the part of most of the denominational officials. Except for the experience in New Haven, in no major city in America has such a wide spectrum of black leadership been brought together as has been done in Newark. Yet much of the interdenominational leadership has not seen fit thus far to have responsible black men set their own agenda. "I's" have been asked to be dotted and "T's" crossed in a way that has not been done for projects that have not led to power for black people or for church projects among black people that have been white-led.

One of the worst civic rebellions in our history has come and gone in Newark. Business goes on as usual. White people with open and sympathetic minds are needed. However, the white Protestant mind-set, as suggested earlier, is not always the most ready asset for black people as they seek to develop authentic power. Leland Stark, the Bishop of Newark, writes:

> In the past we have too often sought simple answers to what have turned out to be hard and complex problems. In this respect the Church has been caught in the same situation as society in general. Being kind and being right are sometimes polar opposites. In order to be right, we must often do something that is painful and open to widespread misunderstanding.
>
> It is painful to risk bad judgments on the part of others whose destinies white people have largely controlled. This is especially the case when denominational executives like myself are asked unilaterally to provide resources, "with no strings attached." It is painful also to be patient while our cities are being torn apart even though we know that quick answers may temporarily ameliorate a critical situation but in the long term may add to our present woes.
>
> Our problem has been complicated further by the fact that in the past black people themselves have sought and have apparently been content with kindness. Only recently have black people begun to seek power to stand on their own and to add their weight to the leadership that is needed to save our cities. This is a healthful development.

Nationally the white Protestant community, in cooperation with Roman Catholic community development agencies, has funded and promoted so-called community organization among the "ghetto poor." These agencies, with the best of goodwill, have not appeared to perceive that black people are not in a poor box but in a box that is colored black. These religious groups, often unconsciously, have added to the fragmenting of the black community by building neighborhood power blocs at the very time that black people have needed to see their problems whole and have needed to work together for black group power in the total metropolitan or political areas of which they are a part.

The churches of our cities may bring regeneration to their own internal life by seeking to deal far more realistically than they have been disposed to do in the past with problems in the life of our cities. Our churches—along with other civic institutions—to a large extent have not been basically geared or committed to critical change. In Chapter V we shall look more closely at several aspects of the role of civic and educational institutions in relation to social change. The simple understanding of their unconscious role as effective guardians of the status quo should provide new insight, and possibly the basis for new life, for our urban churches as well. This suggests that the churches and other institutions in our central cities may have far more to gain than to give from an open-minded and self-giving spirit in the face of our mounting urban distress.

During and after the Newark uprising, the Reverend Richard Schoolmaster, Chairman of the Department of Urban Work of the Episcopal Diocese of Newark and Rector of Grace Church, Orange, New Jersey, sought to interpret to his suburban parishioners their relationship to the city. "We treat our cities in much the same way that we treat black people," he told his congregation. "Unconsciously we ride on their backs. Every opportunity which we or our parents have had has been enhanced and accompanied by the arbitrary exclusion of black people from like opportunities. Thus no matter what our personal feelings may be, we all benefit from our society's overall limitation of black people. None of us can fully make up for this. It is much the same situation with our cities. Unconsciously we ride on their backs. We use them to make our livings and for their cultural assets, but we don't want to share in their problems. Furthermore we both arrange for and allow many of our problem people—the old, the lame, the halt and the blind—to become the charges of our cities. When we realize how good and pleasant our suburban life is and thank God for it, the city pays for the prayers we pray."

By the time these lines are read some new situations may prevail for those concerned with organization of the black community in and around the City of Newark. Even as I write a master design for Newark, modelled after insights soon to be set forth in my *Programs for Power*, is being formulated with the cooperation of civic, business and religious groups. Lessons must be learned daily at every hand. One thing seems certain. Black people of responsibility must be single-minded in their efforts. They must see their problems whole and work cooperatively to the fullest extent possible in the light of long-standing realities. Open rebellions may recur but the basic problems of our cities and of black people remain. Hasty answers in response to emergency needs are no effective antidote to the condition of continuing near riot that marks our cities.

4. Unplanned Exploitation: The Economic Gap

Unplanned exploitation of the cities on the part of the suburbs and the nation has occurred not only through the concentration in the cities of people with problems. Unintended exploitation has also occurred through inequities in employment patterns and in faulty planning for the so-called "ghetto poor."

RECEIVING THE DEBTS OF OTHERS

William Mercer, Coordinator of Newark's Business and Industrial Coordinating Council, writes: "So great is the employment gap between city and suburbs, meaning in Newark black and white, that although our agency is said to be the best of its type in the nation we must do our level best simply to keep from getting more and more behind."

Newark's Business and Industrial Coordinating Council was formed in July 1963 as the result of a protest by civil rights organizations against discrimination in the building trade unions. The

78

leading employers in Newark's Central Business District were asked to associate themselves with the civil rights protest or themselves face a demonstration. The employers refused to comply and instead they organized a committee to open employment opportunities to black people in their own firms. This later became the Business and Industrial Coordinating Council, commonly called the "BICC."

At present the BICC includes some one hundred fifty companies in Greater Newark, along with representatives of civil rights groups, social agencies, labor unions, public agencies, the clergy, and other civic interest groups. The agency provides a forum for broad-based discussion generally relating to the employment conditions of black people. The agency has an excellent reputation for integrity and dedication. It has not succeeded in making even a beginning at *closing the economic gap* between black and white people in Greater Newark. The same general condition prevails, even if to a less pronounced degree, throughout the country. The pattern of suburban and national exploitation of the cities is well-nigh universal.

As of July 1967, the following employment picture existed for Newark.

1. While 80 percent of Newark's jobs were white collar, only 3.7 percent of these were held by black people. Again, 80 percent of these white collar jobs were held by commuting suburbanites.
2. Only 7.9 percent of the blue collar jobs, skilled and unskilled, were held by black people.
3. The major "fair employment" employee, the federal government, had only 14 percent of its positions held by black people.
4. Only 10.5 percent of all the jobs in the twenty-one largest companies in Greater Newark were held by black people.

There are more statistics, but some breathing space must be afforded by a commentary on these staggeringly tragic indicators of distress. In spite of all the efforts concentrated on Newark, Manuel Diaz, Regional Director of the federal Equal Employment Opportunities Commission, could comment on August 7, 1967, that

"Newark is the most dramatic situation—negatively—I've run into in terms of equal opportunity." He added: "I've gotten the feeling that some of the key people in this town—who have the most power—have gone back to business as usual. The attitude is 'let BICC take care of it.' It's a sad attitude and something has to be done to change it."

Mr. Diaz' comments are revealing in an ironic way. The federal government itself has power. It seeks to bring about change in the employment practices of private employers. Yet Newark, with a black population majority of possibly 55 to 70 percent, has its black population represented on the federal employment roles by only 14 percent. This is further underscored by the unofficial role of the federal government as traditional employer of last resort for black people. The federal government first needs to learn that we cannot be effective change agents unless we are willing to be changed ourselves.

Further, since conditions throughout the nation have forced the migration of black people into our central cities, the federal government should, as an evidence of rudimentary responsibility, assure the equitable distribution of the nation's migrant, unskilled poor or take the initiative in the development of devices that will prevent local communities from unduly bearing problems generated in other parts of the nation.

It is patently unfair for Mississippi, Alabama, South Carolina, or any other state with depressed communities to export, either by overt or covert measures, their problem people and expect the already overburdened cities to bear the responsibilities for their employment, maintenance, education, or rehabilitation. The fact that provisions are made for financial relief to areas that experience serious financial depression is not a sufficient answer to the problems occasioned by the "free migration" of the poor into the central cities.

Clearly the problem of access to communities involves more than the current issue of open housing. The open roadways for the poor and the dispossessed into our cities mean a national exploitation of the already grossly overburdened people who man and must plan for our cities. The federal government must be honest, imaginative, and aggressive—in ways far different than ever before—in seeking some just solution to this long-standing pattern of exploitation.

Nonetheless, Newark's industries and those of other cities cannot be held altogether blameless, or even guiltless of antisocial behavior. It should long ago have been made clear to every agency in the land, which has the privilege of serving the public for private profit, that to conduct one's business in such a manner as to create or aggravate social problems is a crime against society. Hence, it should be a matter of public policy that the hiring practices of any private or public enterprise must advance the public interest. Otherwise private profits are made at social costs for which the taxpayers of the land must pay.

That the employers of Newark have exploited the city by aggravating the social costs borne most immediately by the city's taxpayers left behind by the flight to the suburbs is evident from the following statistics:

1. Newark's largest businesses, the chemical industries, employ only 6.7 percent black people. New Jersey is the largest chemical and pharmaceutical center in the nation. It is a two and one-half billion dollar annual industry. Only 2.1 percent of the black labor force in Greater Newark's chemical industry are white collar workers.
2. In the electrical industries, 10.3 percent of the work force is black.
3. In the insurance business 5.4 percent of the work force is black. This percentage has been static for eighteen years, while other occupational categories were experiencing an average, and far too meager, 8 percent rise in the hiring of black people and other minorities.

These industries are represented in the leadership of the Business and Industrial Coordinating Council. To meet any of the leaders of these industries is an experience. One sees wisdom, vision, and the capacity to get things done. Yet the total efforts of these great captains of industry have done hardly more than meet a growing skills deficiency in their own concerns.

The government's reaction to the effectively vicious employment practices in and about our cities is the equivalent of wringing one's hands in the face of an unwanted pregnancy. More and more resources for the wringing of one's hands will not stop the birth of the baby. So it is with the federal government's patent unwillingness to come to serious grips with the mounting and unreversed pattern of unemployment in our central cities.

The New Jersey state employment office has let many instances of employer discrimination go unpunished so as not to "infringe upon the functions of the anti-discrimination agencies," director of the Newark office admits. To allow business to add wantonly to social burdens is to demonstrate an incapacity to uphold a public trust. The cities must pay the costs of the failure of federal functions. Riots in the cities have already begun. Sabotage in the suburbs may be in the offing. Nor is there an end in sight.

The federal government's major answer to the awesome rape of the cities is a model cities' program, the total budget of which would scarcely do for Newark, even if the program were properly conceived. Its emphasis is upon curing physical blight, with a tip of the hat to human rehabilitation. It seeks to deal with communities burdened with the needs of black people, and solicits "neighborhood" insight. The black people who are faced with rock-bottom needs do not normally live next door to their natural leaders.

The lack of federal government good faith toward compensation to the cities for its share in their exploitation should be evident from the fact that two billion dollars is spent annually on roads and airports. Columnist Joseph Alsop reports: "This annual outlay ... equals the entire sum spent on public housing subsidies in the last 17 years."

The one ingredient lacking is the will and determination of the persons most responsible for the federal trust. To claim to be one's friend or ally and to overlook or withhold repayment of an honest debt or responsibility makes a mockery of one's profession. But everyone seems to have entered the act. The games we all share would almost be hilarious in retrospect, if they were not so tragic for America. Look, for example, at what those with admitted compassion do for the inequitable burdens created by the presence of the cities' poor.

POVERTY OR POWER?

The most imaginative response given in recent history to the problem of poverty has been the federal antipoverty program under the Office of Economic Opportunity. In the past, we have had massive poverty; and the government's response was to give the poor an investment in the nation's life through the offer of free land. The government has also done what was tantamount to giving free suburban homes to aspiring white people by subsidizing their home ownership under the FHA for proportionately less than what it has cost black people to be kept as perpetual tenants in our central cities.

The federal antipoverty program seeks to make the poor self-sustaining. It seeks to avoid welfare colonialism by the provision of the "maximum feasible participation of the poor" in local programs launched to meet the needs of local people. If white people are poor, it is largely because they lack skills and need training. The poverty of black people is not due primarily to lack of skills or education or work experience, which is the focus of the antipoverty efforts. *The poverty of black people is due chiefly to the group's low status and lack of power in national life.*

Whenever black people are trained, they are trained largely for frustration. Bureau of the Census figures in the *Statistical Abstract of the United States* indicate clearly what has been a continuing national pattern. More than 70 percent of the disparity between black and non-black income for more than a decade has been due to causes other than education or training. Ernest Erber of the New Jersey Committee of the Regional Plan Association points to the basic issue behind the relative difficulty of attainment on the part of every black man: It is "the inferior status to which he is relegated by the rest of society." Unless we address ourselves to the status-power problem for black people, we cannot hope to close what the National Urban League speaks of as "the unclosing gap" between black and white Americans.

Can the federal government aid black people in developing status, group pride, and sufficient group power so that the desperately hopeless will be motivated to other than dependency and despair? What could the Office of Economic Opportunity do, other than trying to approach poverty as it has done?

The first question is answered broadly in what follows. In answer to the second question, it is doubtful that the Office of Economic Opportunity could have done—in the early 1960's—anything other than what it has done. The entire nation was under the illusion that "poverty" was "poverty," no matter who happened to be poor. But black poverty has a built-in burden that is sufficiently limiting as to make it qualitatively a different problem. The approaches of the Office of Economic Opportunity—as those of all of our federal agencies—ought to have been marked, and openly dealt with, as "tentative."

Christopher Jenks and David Riesman put their finger firmly on the problem that must be dealt with directly by black men themselves. The federal government, however, must help to discover or develop devices by which to encourage or force the hands of black men to come to grips with that interior problem, the solution to which is crucial to the nation. Jenks and Riesman in the statement below may seem to some to be attacking unduly the colleges of black people. But listen to the basic message about the inevitable results of an absence of ethnic pride in terms of its broadest possible implications.

The Negro colleges had no such quarrel with Anglo-American culture. Mostly they were founded by whites, financed by whites, and at least in their early years administered and staffed mainly by whites. . . . Instead of trying to promote a distinctive set of habits and values in their students, they were, by almost any standard, purveyors of super-American, ultra-bourgeois prejudices and aspirations. Far from fighting to preserve a separate sub-culture, as (white) ethnic colleges did, the Negro colleges were militantly opposed to almost everything which made Negroes different from whites. . . . The Negro colleges . . . were separate only because the white colleges which they emulated would not admit their students.

Under such circumstances, the Negro colleges could have maintained their self-respect only if they had viewed themselves as a pre-revolutionary holding operation, designed to salvage the victims of injustice. This stance would, however, have demanded an open and continual attack on segregation and white supremacy, which the Negro colleges could not afford to make. The result was usually self-contempt, born either from acceptance of the white view that Negroes were inferior or from disgust at having succumbed silently to an outrageous injustice, or from both.

The cumulative result of all this was that the Negro college of the 1950's was usually an ill-financed, ill-staffed caricature of white higher education . . .[1]

This image of black-institutions is a mirror of the American image of black men on the basis of which our status or place in the nation is determined.

Our marginal status as black men in American life should equip us to be the most useful and creative agents for the nation. Yet we all too often act in terms of the inferior roles proposed for us, when self-respecting black men with integrity and discernment must do only what is good for the country. Gifted, authentic black men must offer the Office of Economic Opportunity, and all the agencies of commerce in our land, the benefits of their unique historical and cultural experience, where they have been afforded a kind of dramatic distance to view conditions with potentially saving perspective.

In the City of Newark the antipoverty program is credited with being one of the best administered in the country. Cyril Tyson, its original administrator, admits that the thrust of his brief tenure was administrative. Only as he was about to leave his work in Newark did he have time to begin to raise serious questions about the propriety of some of the Office of Economic Opportunity's efforts.

Faced with Newark's almost unparalleled black poverty, the United Community Corporation, Newark's antipoverty agency, in its "Program Report 1966–67," lists twelve enterprises that make up its answer to local poverty needs. They are grouped under three headings. The first is education.

ANTIPOVERTY APPROACHES: EDUCATION

(a) **Newark Pre-School Council Inc.** This is an ably administered program, with built-in leverages to involve the parents, providing three thousand children with their first learning experience, on a year-round basis.

Privately, administrators in this program admit to the basic inability to deal with any urban-induced problem by beginning

[1] *Harvard Educational Review*, January, 1967.

with children. Fundamentally, urban problems are not generated in the childhood environment. Urban problems come by accretion, from without and through the adult environment. Studies of preschool programs throughout the country indicate a reversion tendency on the part of the pupils, due to the adverse influence of the home and community environment in which the children must live. If the parents, rather than the children of preschool age, are dealt with in terms of their own educational growth, two crucial things will happen for the regeneration of our cities. The parents themselves will be *empowered* to deal with their own children's problems, and there will be an *immediate* change in the home environment in terms of the value placed upon learning. This raises the question of the type of rehabilitative education that may be best suited for adults in the city. We shall deal with this in some detail in Chapter V.

(b) **High School Head Start and (c) Upward Bound.** High School Head Start is an award-winning program of UCC, started in 1965 and designed to prepare students about to enter high school in reading, mathematics, language skills, music, and art. Upward Bound is a similar program for precollege students. In 1966, 211 students took part in High School Head Start, while 140 students took part in Upward Bound.

Let us look at something of the situation to which these two programs were addressed, as set forth in a flyer prepared by those responsible for Newark's "Crusade For Learning":

The 1965 graduating class of Central High School had started with 654 young people in the 10th grade. By June of 1965, 310 had dropped out of school. Of the graduating class of 344, 79 young people sought higher education. What has happened to the 575 students who were forced to seek employment either before or immediately after graduation? In this situation we cannot afford to be indifferent to the conditions in our schools.

Prevailing conditions in the schools and in the adult environment would appear to be the basic points at which the problems of these young people should be attacked. Of every ten black people in Newark, 8.5 do not have high school diplomas. Some came to Newark without diplomas. The system is producing others.

Civil rights leaders and white civic leaders in the City of Newark have spoken more openly since the July rebellion about apparent repressive attitudes on the part of teachers and administrators in the Newark schools. School officials will not admit to racial biases or to the influence even of the prejudicial cultural assumptions that are nationally pervasive. It should be recognized in an open and honest way that in our culture—as it is, and has been—racism has its highly valued place. Hence, even black people, in trying to identify with the dominant culture, tend to hate and persecute themselves. Is it reasonable to assume that white people will ever be led to do anything less?

Antipoverty programs, directed at offsetting problems deeply imbedded in understandable ways in the well-intentioned Newark schools, are like the administering of local anesthesia to a tumor. The problem must be approached from within. The teachers and administrators in the system, however kindly disposed, are products of or are related to the escapist and exploitative syndrome that characterizes the white ring of entrenchment around the city or are related to the suburban haven that has harbored those who unconsciously exploit the city.

Can such people as these, without the deepest self-understanding and a fundamental reorientation of their way of life, hope to teach the young people whose very presence in our cities symbolizes the destruction and devaluation of a world that the teachers and administrators have highly prized? This seems unreasonable at a glance. The record of the school system in not halting drop-outs tells its undeniable tale. The following resolution adopted by the Newark Commission on Human Rights, June 7, 1967, also reveals the mind-set of the system that seeks to bring fulfillment and growth into maturity and hope for the black youth of the City of Newark. The resolution reads:

WHEREAS the Newark Board of Education has denied non-white, non-instructional employees the opportunity to fill temporary vacancies in the office of Assistant Superintendent of Special Services within the Board of Education Administration building and such vacancies were filled by persons from outside the Board of Education Administration building;

WHEREAS non-white employees have been told that they cannot receive the maximum salary of the job they are temporarily filling if the person they are replacing is on sick leave but still carried on the payroll, yet this regulation has not been adhered to if the person temporary filling such vacancy is not non-white;

WHEREAS in the Child Guidance department, Newark Board of Education, two Clerk Stenographers hired in September 1966; the non-white was hired as a temporary (no benefits) and the other Clerk Stenographer (not even a resident of Newark) was given a Provisional status (all benefits);

WHEREAS in the office of the Board of Education Counsel all Senior Clerk Stenographers including non-white Senior Clerk Stenographers were asked if they were interested in filling a vacancy of Legal Stenographer. When only three of the Senior Clerk Stenographers (all-non-white) indicated such interest they were told that they were not qualified;

WHEREAS a vacancy of Clerk-Stenographer in the Superintendent's office occurred in September 1966. A non-white Clerk-Stenographer indicated interest in filling this vacancy. She was denied the job and a High school graduate with no experience was placed in this job and at a Provisional status;

WHEREAS a non-white Senior Clerk Stenographer in the Business Administration office requested her supervisor to give her the opportunity to fill a vacancy of six months (Principal Clerk Stenographer) yet she has been denied this opportunity although she has been performing all duties of Principal Clerk Stenographer;

WHEREAS a non-white employee, a graduate of an Electronics Institute, has been denied the opportunity to work as a Computer operator in spite of a directive from the Office of the Secretary to the Board of Education that he be given this opportunity;

WHEREAS there are no non-white personal secretaries in any of the offices of the Assistant Superintendents;

WHEREAS the City of Newark represents a city of 55% non-whites and a school population of 78% non-white;

WHEREAS there has not been one non-white person in a policy making position on the Newark Board of Education in 300 years;

WHEREAS there has only been 1 non-white principal in the Newark school system in one hundred years;

WHEREAS in the Office of the Superintendent there are no non-whites in policy making positions;

WHEREAS in the Personnel Department there are no non-whites at a Supervisory or Administrative level.

WHEREAS in the Practical Arts Dept. there are no non-whites in Supervisory or Administrative positions;

WHEREAS in the Health Dept. there are no non-whites in Supervisory or Administrative positions;

WHEREAS in the Cafeteria Dept. there are no non-whites in Supervisory or Administrative positions;

WHEREAS in the Adult Education Dept. there are no non-whites in Supervisory or Administrative positions (no non-white clerical);

WHEREAS in the Attendance Dept. there are no non-whites in Supervisory or Administrative positions;

WHEREAS in the Child Guidance Dept. there are no non-white Psychiatrists;

WHEREAS in the Reference and Research Dept. there are no non-whites in Supervisory or Administrative positions;

WHEREAS in the Business Administration Dept. there are no non-whites in Supervisory or Administrative positions;

WHEREAS in the Recreation and Physical Education Dept. there are no non-whites in the Supervisory or Administrative positions (no non-white clerical);

WHEREAS in the Depository Dept. there are no non-whites in Supervisory or Administrative positions;

WHEREAS in the Purchasing Dept. there are no non-whites in Supervisory or Administrative positions;

WHEREAS under TITLE 18:25–12 LAW AGAINST DISCRIMINATION Unlawful employment practice or unlawful discrimination
It shall be an unlawful employment practice, or, as the case may be, an unlawful discrimination for an employer to "discriminate against such individual in compensation or in terms, conditions or privileges of employment";

WHEREAS the Newark Human Rights Commission does not have the power of subpoena;

WHEREAS it is necessary that certain records and documents in the possession need to be examined;

WHEREAS it is necessary to receive testimony from those persons in positions of authority and policy making within the Board of Education;

THEREFORE be it resolved that the Newark Human Rights Commission request immediately of the New Jersey Division on Civil Rights, Department of Law and Public Safety to investigate the past and present employment and upgrading policies regarding non-white professional, non-professional, Administrative and Supervisory personnel within the Newark Board of Education.

[signed] ALBERT BLACK
CHAIRMAN

June 7, 1967

Since the above resolution, one black person has been named an assistant superintendent for curriculum and three other black persons added to the administrative staff. Five white persons were upgraded at the same time to relatively higher positions. Significantly, the gap in relative employment levels for white and black is not being closed in a substantial way. *The closing of the gap between black people and others must be the critical factor by which every enterprise dealing with the needs of black people is gauged.*

In the antipoverty program for Newark several other educational programs, through (*d*) *The Child Service Association,* (*e*) *The Fuld Neighborhood House,* and (*f*) *The Hilary School,* approach the problem of poverty from the environment of childhood. Poverty is foisted upon the cities through forces at work in the adult environment. These adult environmental factors must be identified and changed.

ANTIPOVERTY APPROACHES: MANPOWER

This is the second area of project focus of the antipoverty program in Newark.

(a) **On-Job-Training.** This program is reported to have served 263 persons since operations began in February 1967. The UCC report for 1966–67 reads: "The program is a vehicle by which many disadvantaged and underemployed people can *advance themselves* through the acquisition of new and more critically needed skills. By screening applicants UCC *provides a much-needed service to* *the businessman looking for dependable workers."* (Italics mine.) The first italics suggest that the program is aimed at those who are basically self-directed. The major need in our efforts to eliminate or reduce poverty is to deal with those who are not self-directed.

Let us look at this program and at the other programs immediately below in the light of the needs to which they seek to address themselves. There are ten thousand unemployed and out-of-school youth between the ages of seventen and twenty-one alone in the City of Newark. This does not speak of the underemployed or of those with potential for reentry into schooling for traditional higher education.

An unconsciously provided clue to the unintended exploitative nature of the program is suggested by the second italicized phrase. The total thrust of all of the employment efforts for black people in Newark has done hardly more than provide "a much-needed service to businessmen." Certainly the task of closing the gap has not begun in any substantial or apparently continuing way. Black leaders caught up in the present programs freely admit to this. Even they are exploited.

(b) Career Oriented Preparation for Employment (COPE) and (c) The Blazer Community Employment Training Program service manpower needs of the city. To suggest that they are not needed is like indicating that provision for drainage is not necessary for a mountain wall. But the drainage does not build the wall.

In 1967, according to the UCC annual report, some twenty-five hundred youths came through COPE's doors. Three hundred fifty enrollees were recruited for COPE's project. Of these, one hundred took permanent positions and one hundred were returned to school. Eighty agencies, public and private, are hiring the one hundred who are permanently employed.

The Blazer enterprise, according to the UCC report, "launched a training program with courses in auto repair, upholstery, floor maintenance, and food service. . . . Blazer also provides remedial classes for its enrollees and an on-site day care center for their children." The Blazer enterprise, among the manpower projects, is perhaps the most exciting in the involvement of its constituents in planning. Some two hundred Newark residents are being helped by the Blazer program. Much of this is due to the charismatic leadership of its director, Walter Dawkins. In a pamphlet describing the work of the Blazer Coordinating Council, Mr. Dawkins writes:

There should be little doubt in the hearts and minds of all free men that one can seldom deny the basic human rights of his fellowman, without himself becoming less free. The piteous proof of the preceding statement is the most obvious fact that suppressed people throughout the entire world are in revolt against those who would deprive the individual of his basic right to share in the progress and profit of his social environment.

The degree to which any people will suffer and endure the misery of poverty, disease and degradation is, in the final analysis, dependent upon how well those who would dare oppress, meet their basic human needs.

Burned deep in the hearts, souls, and minds of the unfortunate, frustrated, poverty stricken men and women, who by day and night walk the desolate, barren streets and alleys of Newark, New Jersey, is the daily terror of poverty. It was during December, 1962, that the Blazer Enterprises first extended to this lost economic and social group a ray of hope, and a warm hand of friendship. The Enterprise has since become the Blazer Coordinating Council of Youth Development, a non-profit corporation designed and constructed to open the door of opportunity for the thousands who languish at the bottom of the social and economic ladder.

The Blazer Coordinating Council of Youth Development is an organization inspired by the youth and adults of Clinton Avenue and the South Ward Community. When first we presented our one-point program to the public, we were overwhelmed by the response of some four hundred teenagers and adults.

In the City of Newark there are many older residents who are poor and do not clearly understand how the Economic Opportunity Act can really aid them. They see that most of the programs that are developing, and those that they read about, involve youth between the ages of sixteen and twenty-one. Part of the reason for this program is to reach those individuals who are poor, over twenty-one, and with no marketable skills.

The idealism of a Walter Dawkins is representative of the antipoverty efforts throughout the nation at their best. But idealism, without a clear and accurate vision of the task, cannot save America. The Ford Foundation study of several antipoverty projects, released in September 1967, reports the utter failure of such efforts as the job corps, work experience and neighborhood youth corps to move effectively toward their hoped for goals. There is scant evidence that any of the above programs—however well-liked or well-administered they may be—are even remotely tied to the roots of poverty as they are manifested in the City of Newark.

Further, so much of Newark's poverty is tied to a pattern of urban exploitation. To prepare the poor of Newark for marginal, marketable skills will not close the hitherto unclosing economic gap. In many ways any efforts at training for those ripe for exploitation is preparation for further frustration. This is clearly evident in the aborted efforts of those of the greatest goodwill and power in Newark at changing patterns even in those enterprises they control. The UCC programs, after raising the hopes of the poor, can only dash them. It is a delicate and dangerous thing to quicken the hopes of those who feel that life has left them only a legacy of despair.

In an indirect sense, those among us with goodwill, which was unconsciously expressed in ways devoid of the greatest critical assessment, gave our supply of fuel to the mounting conflagration in our cities. So emotive are we with regard to the rightness of what we would will to be right that we often find effrontery even in the suggestion that in some way unforseen we, too, may have helped make a funeral pyre of Newark, Detroit, Watts, and elsewhere.

ANTIPOVERTY APPROACHES: SPECIAL PROJECTS

This is the third and final category of efforts by Newark's United Community Corporation. Listed in this group are (a) *Golden Age*, (b) *Summer Block Recreation*, (c) *Newark Legal Services Project*, (d) *Project ENABLE, and* (e) the *UCC Small Business Development Center.*

The Golden Age program and Summer Block Recreation are clearly service projects. Project ENABLE also fits into this category, as it largely involves help with family adjustment problems. One hundred forty-five families were reported to have participated and another three hundred fifty-five families were reported to have been contacted and interviewed. The Newark Legal Services Project has done a substantial job in limiting the exploitation of the poor, and, along with the other fine UCC programs, deserves praise for its essential community service.

The UCC Small Business Investment enterprise has come closest of any of the antipoverty projects in Newark to dealing with immediate and continuing economic leverage for the benighted black community. That people should derive the economic benefits from their immediate environment is an assumption involving rudimentary justice. The ownership of small businesses in an urban renewal area has its built-in hazards. The spirit of the Small Business Investment enterprise should be supported by the major business leaders in Newark, so that black businesses would be drawn far more extensively into the Central Business District. Significantly, this project is no longer funded.

The laissez-faire attitude of those who hold economic power in Newark regarding the entry of black businessmen into the CBD was demonstrated recently when a black masonic group sought to purchase the property of the Newark Athletic Club. Banks refused to take the mortgage, in spite of good credit and the offer of an unusually high down payment. Several lending institutions that expressed interest in accepting the mortgage were reminded by other banks with which they did business that lending substantial money to the black group would jeopardize their continuing relations with other banks. Those banks who had expressed interest quickly changed their minds. The property was finally sold to the black masonic group, after great vexation and a more than 50 percent increase in the building's price.

This is common practice in any area where black men seek to break new ground. The same businesses that provide leadership for fair employment committees in Newark and elsewhere turn their backs on most efforts at truly significant change. A black leader of the BICC thus remarked:

If the white business leaders really meant business in terms of closing the economic gap for black people, they would long ago have developed at least a four-point program involving

1. Investment opportunities for black business, and the removal of all present roadblocks for black brokers engaged in insurance and other business.

2. A moratorium on all white personnel upgrading until black men, previously locked out of even opportunity for job consideration, were moved in massive numbers into new positions *according to their present potential.*

3. The initiation of arrangements with the federal government for some national provisions for all business enterprises to assure equitable employment for all in order that business will not add to local social welfare and policing problems.

4. Interest in redirecting the educational enterprise which, by a striking coincidence, experiences a high drop-out rate, especially for black youth, just at the time that less low-skilled workers are needed by business and industry.

That most of the UCC-sponsored programs, however fine their services may be, have any substantial relationship to the elimination of Newark's painful and awesome poverty cannot be demonstrated from either their performance or their design. That new approaches must be made is certain.

NO END IN SIGHT

Still the poor are entering our cities, and their numbers are not likely to abate. Their unintended exploitation was underscored by Jonathan Lindley, deputy assistant secretary of the Economic Development Administration, in a report released in August 1967. Mr. Lindley indicated that "it has been the push of poor rural conditions rather than the pull of urban economic opportunities," that produced the migration of more than ten million persons from rural to urban areas in the 1950–60 decade. He added: "There is every indication that the growth in productivity in agriculture and extractive industries will continue over the next 10 years, and consequently that the migration of people from rural to urban areas will also continue."

It is an unreasonable assumption to believe that the mind conditioned to exploit will seek, even in its compassion, to end the condition of exploitation. It may, however, seek to relieve "tension" or to make our pain more bearable. The powerless black poor are poor primarily because they are powerless and have low status. Only as black people address themselves to the issues of their status and power will power relations in our cities change. Thoughtful white people, who are concerned in a responsible way for the survival and orderly development of the nation, will encourage black people to develop new instruments for effecting such a significant change in approach.

5 Signs of the Times

In and through their present mounting and disconcerting chaos, the cities have a highly necessary and potentially creative role they must play for our survival.

HONEST CONFRONTATION

Our cities are in a unique position to help the nation face deeprooted problems that touch everyone but are evident in a more advanced way for them. The open confrontations are signs of the times. They should help us see how escapism, repression, hostility, and violence of various kinds pervade American life.

People have fled to the suburbs in no small measure to escape hard and bitter realities that are inescapable for those who live in the cities. Those in the city know that dislocation and desecration have become a continuing condition in our common life. The current manifestations of our urban unrest are but a surfacing of deeper restlessness and discontent that stem from and give shape to our society as a whole.

97

People who are fearful lose their equanimity far too easily. The tragically revealing response of the able Governor of New Jersey to the Newark rebellion was more characteristic of the mind-set of the nation than most of would like to believe. Governor Richard Hughes lost the dispassion of a sophisticated man sworn to uphold the public trust when he spoke of the uprising in Newark as a "criminal insurrection." Were this the case, there would be no need for his subsequent appointment of a Governor's Select Commission on Civil Disorders to fathom the roots of unrest.

Harry Ashmore of the Center for the Study of Democratic Institutions in Santa Barbara, California, tells of an unexpected highly emotional response to destruction during the 1965 Watts riots. The reaction came from a man Ashmore describes as "a distinguished Californian who has held high government office and enjoys a deserved reputation as an advocate of racial tolerance and social reform."[1] On seeing a picture of burning and pillage in Watts, he pounded his fists on his knees and shouted: "Damn them all—they're nothing but animals! By God, I never thought I'd say it, but they ought to be sent back to Africa!"

"I never thought *I'd say it* . . ." Apparently the feeling was there all along. As a nation, we have continued to be resentful over what we have considered to be a thorn in the flesh. Wherever black people have made their way into any part of the nation in large numbers, there have been increased social problems. We have dealt with the tensions caused by the problems, but typically we have failed to come to grips with the problems themselves. Black people are problem people. We have helped make them so.

What we do in gross or exaggerated ways for black people we do in some measure for all others in our society. Children in our suburban communities fail to learn because of our unwillingness to allow them to become what their innate potential, as conditioned by their own self-awareness, would suggest they might be. In this sense, we have our home-grown brand of black sheep in almost every sheepfold in America. A special education teacher in a well-to-do suburban community reports that the school in which she teaches has no room set aside for the students with special needs. In spite of the large number of students requiring specialized assistance, the school is unwilling to risk changing its

[1] *New York Post*, September 7, 1967, p. 14.

public image from that of an institution for those who would excel.

Our view of life is limited by our unwillingness to face clear realities. We gauge success by arbitrary standards that are unrelated to the need for helping each person find the fulfillment uniquely proper to him. We assign places and roles out of keeping with personal or national growth into the greatest productiveness and maturity. We do this in a way that is disastrous when we live in times that call for continuing planned and thoughtful change.

Each person has his own contribution to make to our homes, to our communities, and to our nation and world. Our task in relation to others is to encourage every person in our society to become what he or she should be. The growing number of suburban young people whose alienation drives them to seek anonymity and self-expression or a sense of release in the Greenwich Villages of the nation is evidence of our inability or unwillingness to help every life find its own fulfillment.

PRESERVING DIVERSITY

Our latent and occasionally verbalized contempt for black people is but an unconscious manifestation of our contempt for life as we experience it in general. Society tends to seek order, while individual life seeks fulfillment. When the two purposes do not agree, difficulties inevitably follow. So it has been in America. New groups of people have poured in, making constant adjustment a basic condition with which we have had to deal. Had our vision of a "melting-pot" been different from that of puree-production and more in the direction of the creation of a tasty and variegated stew, we would not be faced today with the inevitable frustration that comes from any attempt to make all life alike.

The white people who have come to America are not all alike. Many have kept some semblance of their basic ethnic character and integrity and have continued to greatly enrich our common life. But the uncritically examined predisposition toward conformity is a sad sign; for life at its best involves the continuing unfolding of new possibilities, further enhanced by the interchange that can only come from the persistence of healthy diversity.

In America we have sought to make black people carbon copies of white people. Such a task has been impossible. We could not—or cannot—wish away the crippling effects of centuries of slavery. Nor can we simply wish away the low status and lack of power that the maintenance of a slave mentality of dependence upon others has produced for America's black people as a whole. Until several generations ago, black people may have had to bow to circumstances beyond their seeming control and so depend excessively upon the charity of others. Such has not been the case, however, in recent years. A culturally and historically conditioned perception of helplessness marks off black people in America as different from the rest. This represents a fact of life we cannot afford to gloss over.

Yet we have sought to deal with differences by overlooking them. This is in part a legacy from an unfortunate aspect of liberalism that was evident in the days of Queen Victoria. Victorian liberalism had within its character the regrettable tendency toward seeking to make things good by wishing that they were so. The Victorian of goodwill saw the good in people and in situations at the expense of seeing life situations entire. The deeply religious and compassionate Queen herself could weep for the thousands of her Irish subjects dying from a potato famine and respond with a small contribution from her personal purse.

Post-Victorian liberalism, with respect to black Americans, has tended likewise to confuse hopes with their achievement. Black people have been nurtured for their goal of freedom under the post-Victorian liberal mind. Those possessed of this mind-set had the best intentions. They planned for and protected black people when black people seemed to be in no condition to plan for or protect themselves. Until our present day those of the same white liberal tradition have sought to do all that was in their particular power to bring black people into the center of national life.

LIMITS OF WISHFUL THINKING

The white liberal method of approach, however, included the viewing of reality through tinted glasses. So the effective indolence or abject hopelessness of black people, occasioned in large part by the centuries' long experience of giving one's best efforts for unjustly meager rewards, was ignored. If hopelessness and indolence are not recognized, neither can their causes be faced and dealt with. This is also true of socially inflicted black self-hate and irresponsibility. The glossing over of historically rooted differences between white and black Americans has been one of the basic causes of our failure to make black people into anything other than problem people.

The latent contempt for black people evident in the off-guard statements by Governor Richard Hughes and by the California friend of Harry Ashmore may be understood in some degree, although not justified, by a look at the results of uncritical judgment on the part of black Americans themselves.

Black men and women of apparent success, for example, often buy into the use of the fictitious and self-defeating term "progress" to describe their movement out of the blue collar work categories. In so doing, they mask the need for the creation of new mechanisms or approaches for the attainment of equity by black people in the economics of our country. Table X shows the diminishing number of farm jobs, formerly held by many black people, and the proportionate increase in urban jobs in the white collar category.

TABLE X Labor Force: Percentage Distribution Over Broad Occupation Categories, 1900–1959

CATEGORY	1900	1910	1920	1930	1940	1950	1959
White collar	17.6	21.3	24.9	29.4	31.1	36.6	42.1
Manual and service	44.9	47.7	48.1	49.4	51.5	51.6	48.0
Farm	37.5	30.9	27.0	21.2	17.4	11.8	9.9
Total	100.0	99.9	100.0	100.0	100.0	100.0	100.0

The percentage of workers in the manual and service category remained relatively constant over a sixty-year period. The approximately sixty-year percentage change was only 3.1, from 44.9 percent in 1900 to 48.0 in 1959. Meanwhile the percentage of farm workers moved downward from 37.5 in 1900 to 9.9 in 1959. This represented a drop within the total labor force of 25.6 percent. To turn the statistics around, there were approximately four times as many workers on the farms in 1900 as there were in 1959. The overwhelming majority of all Negroes lived on the farm in 1900. By 1959 the vast preponderance of farm jobs occupied in 1900 simply did not exist.

Negroes moved to the city during this sixty-year period. See Table XI. Farm workers have lower visible income than do nonfarm workers. The shift by Negroes to the city would suggest an apparent economic upgrading for Negroes. In fact the seemingly higher echelon and higher income jobs that Negroes came to occupy in the cities had now become, by a simple change in economic patterns, the lower echelon jobs of 1959.

The most visible sign of apparent economic success on the part of black Americans has been the entry of this group into the ranks of white collar workers. This category of workers represented 17.6 percent of all workers in 1900, but by 1959 this category had more than doubled to 42.1 percent. This represented an inroad of 24.4 percent into the total employment force of the nation. Here again,

TABLE   XI Percentage of Negro and White Population Living in Urban Areas, by Region, Conterminous United States, 1910–60

YEAR	UNITED STATES		SOUTH		NORTH AND WEST	
	NEGRO	WHITE	NEGRO	WHITE	NEGRO	WHITE
1910	27.4	48.7	21.2	23.2	77.5	57.3
1920	35.4	53.3	27.0	28.5	84.3	61.6
1930	43.7	57.6	31.7	35.0	88.1	65.5
1940	48.6	59.0	36.5	36.8	89.1	67.4
1950	62.4	64.3	47.7	48.9	93.5	70.1
1960	73.2	69.6	58.4	58.6	95.3	73.7

SOURCES:
1920–40: Sixteenth Census of the United States: 1940 Population, Vol. II, *Characteristics of the Population*, Pts. 1–7, tables 4, 5, for each state (Bureau of the Census).

1950: Census of Population, 1950, Vol. II, *Characteristics of the Population*, Pt. 1, United States Summary, table 145 (Bureau of the Census).

1960: Census of Population, Detailed Characteristics, United States Summary, Final Report PC (1) 1D, tables 158, 233; 1910: *Abstract of the Thirteenth Census* (1910), table 28, p. 103 (Bureau of the Census).

with automation and technology, nearly one-half the employment force came to be represented in the white collar category. The movement of black Americans into this category by itself may not represent, as often we have been led to believe, an upgrading for black workers, so much as it may reflect a relative downgrading or extension of white collar category jobs.

RESPONSIBILITY AND REFLECTIVE JUDGMENT

Not only has there been an uncritical examination of our economic position as black people; there has also been an unwillingness, until late, for those who are black to speak up with reference to the burdens that the "as is" presence of black people brings to those who must pay for upkeep of the cities.

That one-half of the people on welfare in Newark have lived there less than five years suggests that undue advantage is being taken of our cities. Most of these people whose broad social needs must be provided for, in large measure by white Newark taxpayers, are black. This is true, by and large, in every major American city. The failure of responsible black men to make a serious and objective checking of the score in terms of their own progress has helped undergird the conditions that evoke contempt for black people as a whole.

Few voices calling for reflective judgment on the part of black people in Newark are raised more persistently than that of Mrs. Bernice Bass through her regular Sunday evening radio program of "news and views." One issue on which she sought the concerted interest of the black community is illustrative of the black weaknesses we have alluded to. In September 1967 the Newark City Council approved the expenditure of $625,000 to add to the construction costs of an Ironbound Recreation Center. This brought the total costs of the center to $4.9 million, considerably above the original $1.8 million for the project. The Ironbound Recreation Center is designed to replace the Memorial Stadium, which is being razed to make way for industrial development. The final plans for the Ironbound Recreation Center include the addition of a basketball arena and an ice skating rink. While these facilities will be open to all, and while some playground expansion was planned at the same time for the Central Ward, the predominantly black communities of the city still suffer from proportionately fewer recreational facilities.

Mrs. Bass warned of the increasing disproportion and the finer quality of recreation facilities being provided for the predominantly white areas of the city as symbolized by the fresh additions to the planned center in the largely white Ironbound community. The result: The record reveals that no one spoke at the public hearing on the $625,000 increase for the Ironbound Recreation Center. This pattern of failure to coalesce in continuing ways marks the life of practically every black community throughout the land.

Black people have not insisted that the across-the-board gap be closed between the benefit levels of white and black Americans. This same tragic trend was underscored in a Newark Business and Industrial Coordinating Council report by Dr. Leo Troy, Professor of Economics at Rutgers. In the face of the staggering need for employment of black people *at all levels*, and especially the higher levels, in the business, industrial and public life of Newark according to present potential, the BICC report emphasized the alleged breakthrough in employment with the following claim:

BICC's employment project became so successful, that it is not an exaggeration to claim that the Urban League's employment office has become an extension of the personnel offices of many important Newark area firms. The success of the employment project led the State Employment Service to station a representative at the Urban League's office to advise applicants of the facilities available at The State Employment Service.

What kind of jobs did Negroes and Puerto Ricans get, as a result of the cooperation of the BICC and Urban League? A number of significant job breakthroughs were reported by the Urban League. *Leading in the glamour job area is air-line hostess.* Breakthroughs were also made in the occupations of aircraft and engine mechanic, food salesman, drug detail man, air-line freight agent, bank teller, mortgage analyst, engineers and technicians, clinical investigator (for a drug company), and chemist. Some unusual new occupations which are really first for nonwhites are *model maker* in a toy factory (a very sensitive security job!) and a *security man* on the bus (one who checks on the integrity of the bus drivers).

Small wonder, with this kind of yardstick for progress in closing the economic gap, that we have experienced what we have.

"If I were white and I lived in Newark, I'd riot," so the columnist Jimmy Breslin is reported to have remarked. But neither black nor white people seem open to the facing of the serious disparities and inequities in the nation's life which, if faced, would provoke either insanity on one hand or the aggressive determination to work for thoughtful planned change in our cities on the other.

Pete Hamill, in the *New York Post* on July 31, 1967, just two weeks after the Newark rebellion, alluded to the condition of contempt for life that marks our central cities. His comments must be taken as a fair warning:

The young Negroes who have abandoned hope and taken to the sniper's nest did not need to go very far to learn about violence. If they came from the American South, their fathers lived with it every minute of the day. If they moved North with their families, or were born in the ghettos, they took lessons in violence every evening. In New York, the greatest city in the richest country in history, they learned that the Mafia can drop you in the river with impunity. If they watch TV or read the newspapers, they can hear public servants with distinguished credentials explain how they are bringing peace and tranquility to Southeast Asia by maintaining an efficient kill ratio.

Now Lyndon Johnson has assembled a commission to investigate the causes of the riots and disturbances in the great American cities. Is there anything really to investigate? Anyone who lives in a city knows what causes these things. You do not need 11 members of the Establishment to explain that. People burn down ghettos because they are intolerable places to live in. They loot stores because they live in a country where every medium is mobilized to make them want things like TV sets, radios, whisky, cigarets and clothes: the same country does not provide enough jobs paying enough money to make those things possible.

"If I were white and I lived in Newark, I'd riot," my friend Jimmy Breslin said the other day, and he was right, of course. The Irish rioted in New York during the Civil War because they were being cheated and lied to and abused by the Government and when the riots were over there were 1,200 dead Irishmen. But when the smoke had settled and the dead were buried, the Irish were finally accepted as citizens of this country. It does not behoove their grandchildren in Queens to call the black revolutionaries animals and rabble for using the same tactics.

If the President's commission is honest it will come to one simple conclusion: That we can no longer afford to spend billions of dollars on a smelly little war in Southeast Asia while our cities are rotting and kids in our own country are taking to the gun and to the torch.

Yesterday, Herman Badillo, the Bronx Borough president, said over breakfast that even if the war ended tomorrow he didn't think all the billions would be given to the cities. "The mood of the country isn't running that way," he said. I hope he is wrong. Because if he is right, Detroit and Newark are only the beginning.

We are edgy throughout the nation and understandably so. Men who will not search for solid ground will always be uncertain of where they stand. Our inability to look critically at or to deal constructively with the roots of distress, as expressed most clearly in the life of the black people in our cities, is symptomatic of our national predisposition toward wishful thinking. It is consistent with a failure to deal with harsh realities in other aspects of our society.

Our inability or unwillingness to come to terms with unavoidable problems is reflected further in such diverse ways as the increasing incidence of mental disease and in our present failure to see civic rebellion in the light of the lessons of history. Wherever people have been unduly oppressed they have turned toward escapism or toward rebellion. Thus Plato's *Republic* (Book VIII) speaks of those who see themselves as unjustly poor, plundered or dispossessed as prone to be "in love with revolution." Again, St. Thomas More writes in his *Utopia* (Book I): "Who is bolder in stirring up revolution in the hope of gain from some source or other than the man who now has nothing to lose?" Yet we have the least trained persons on the public payroll advising us in critical areas of public policy where great minds through the ages have spoken with some measure of light.

Our hesitation to face life and death concerns is reflected in our city tax rates that soar recklessly while some complain. But far too few among us are alarmed. Newark's highest proportionate urban tax rate simply suggests where the major cities of the nation are headed. Table XII gives a sampling of Newark's mounting tax impossibilities.

The tax rate of the City of Newark has tripled since 1945, and the needs of the cities continue to mount. The tax problems of Newark reflect parallel financial needs in a growing number of middle-income suburban communities. Thus near the outer ring of every major metropolitan area are new towns or greatly enlarged

TABLE XII   Newark Tax Rates 1945–67

YEAR	RATE (PER $100 OF ASSESSED VALUATION)
1945	$ 5.16
1946	5.56
1947	5.98
1948	6.50
1949	6.76
1950	6.85
1951	6.92
1952	7.79
1954	8.85
1955	8.47
1956	8.43
1957	8.93
1958–60	10.25
1961	10.11
1962	10.75
1963	11.60 (adjusted to previous formula, now changed)
1964	13.20 ” ” ” ” ” ”
1965	12.94 ” ” ” ” ” ”
1966	11.94 (with the use of surplus reserves)
1967	15.52 (adjusted as in 1963)

old towns that find themselves in financial distress. Caught with mortgages and with commuting and other rising costs that over-tax their limited budgets, the householders in these communities are now facing the prospect of higher financial demands on the part of their towns for schools, road and sewerage construction and maintenance and other administrative services. Having left the city to escape one holocaust, these newcomers to the suburbs now face an unrelenting financial "hot seat."

THE ROLE OF VALUES

During the four days of the Newark rebellion, when twenty-eight lives were lost, a reporter observed in a matter-of-fact manner that the intensity of the rebellion increased when bullets began to be used for the purpose of restoring order. It is a strange commentary on our way of life that where official violence increases recklessness, then the greater the recklessness, the more official violence is sanctioned in the public mind. But perhaps the commentary is not so strange after all. As Floyd McKissick reminds us, those who framed the Declaration of Independence and wrote our Constitution believed that human life and property were one. With the official abolition of slavery and the adoption of the amendments guaranteeing the humanity of black people, the value system of the nation did not automatically change. The fact is that we have not, in any thoroughgoing or systematic way, sought to restructure our institutional practices to conform to a lofty conception of the value of human life. We have responded slowly, sporadically, and reluctantly and only under demands reinforced by some substantial threat to internal tranquility.

The matter of human worth lies behind the growing concern for women's rights. It is the issue behind the mounting tensions in upper-class homes and in the schools of suburbia as well as of the central city. What are policemen, firemen, and other public— along with private—employees to be paid? Under what conditions shall men work? What continuing education must be provided for all adults? What about abortion, birth control, capital punishment, and population planning? What kind of housing should we build? What types of jobs are to be fitted to what people and why? What place must public welfare continue to play in urban life? These are all questions which involve, at rock bottom, the matter of human worth.

Presidents Dwight D. Eisenhower and John F. Kennedy were right in their repeated emphasis upon the need for the nation to come to terms with its system of basic values. *Unless our value system is reckoned with, in an immediate or thoroughly substantial way, our nation will continue to move crazily from crisis to crisis, and even greater chaos and inequities will ensue.*

This is true because our view of what life is gives basic shape to every enterprise we commit ourselves to. The abortiveness of planning efforts for our cities—and indeed, even our failure to plan with the comprehensiveness or seriousness of purpose that we should—may be traced in no small way to conflicts and inadequacies in the assumptions that underlie our approach to problems in our personal and common life.

The present crisis in our cities reflects, then, what is far more fundamentally a value crisis. It should be clear that we cannot plan in other than self-defeating ways if we are not agreed upon basic national, local, and domestic goals. The crazy-quilt pattern of relationships created by our lack of comprehensive planning, and which gives some measure of warmth and comfort to some of us, still leaves many others out. How many human lives—and which specific persons in your family or your neighbor's—can we afford to dismiss or to leave out as calculated loss, reckoning over-all success as a society in terms of the law of averages?

PLANNING INGREDIENTS

Assuming a situation where human values are reappraised, what other specific considerations are necessary for effective planning for our cities and for the nation? There are at least four such concerns that have been either overlooked or dealt with inadequately in our past and present approaches to public planning.

1. **Human Growth and Fulfillment.** The most basic value-related problem in our planning efforts is associated with our ultimate end or purpose. Traditionally we have posed an either-or kind of choice. Is our purpose in planning primarily society-oriented? Or is our purpose individually oriented? There is, however, a third, doubtless more valid, choice, particularly for the needs of the changing society of which we shall increasingly be a part. The institutions of our society must be able to foster human growth and fulfillment. Hence, the third, and more relevant question is: How can society facilitate human growth and fulfillment, both individually and collectively? (Incidentally, this last question was the chief concern of the National Conference on Black Power. Such ad hoc meetings, now and in the years to come, can make valuable contributions by encouraging the kind of self-examination so necessary for black Americans.)

If human growth and fulfillment is our basic purpose in planning, then we must look not so much to the *improvement* of institutions in our society as to their *redirection*.

Institutions become institutions by their commitments to the public good. No movement is ever permitted by a society to exist long enough to become an institution unless it demonstrates a willingness and capacity to uphold the public good "as is." The technical name for "the public good as is" is mores, meaning the public morality. Morals, in this root sense, represent the perceived immediate interests of those presently in power. Morals change only when there is a basic change in relationships of power.

All of our civic, educational, religious, and business institutions are committed to uphold the public morality. Their basic purpose with respect to society is to help to create or to maintain stability. Institutions, structurally, tend to be repressive, in the sense that their basic dynamic is toward providing society with a ballast.

To look for recreation from within our present institutions is like hunting for fish in the sky. The facilitation of basically needed change is not a function natural to institutions. Yet institutions, if *they are aware* of their normal dynamics and mindful of the absolute necessity of change for the nation's survival, may yet serve a crucial role in America's present urgent hour. Failing this, there may be little hope for our continuing growth *as the kind of society to which we have been committed.*

In the next two chapters we shall discuss three specific issues that have frustrated the most serious attempts of our public and private institutions to bring about highly necessary change. But the fact that human growth and fulfillment in Newark, for example, is not being achieved is made clear by the growing proportion of Newark residents on the public welfare roles. Nearly one-half the black children in Newark Public Schools come from homes permanently subsidized through the public welfare.

Douglas Eldridge, staff writer for the *Newark News*, wrote on January 29, 1967, of the apparently endless spiraling of relief costs. The tragic story is a variation on a well-nigh universal urban theme. Human life is not being prepared to grow into the capacity to maintain itself. Indeed we have not planned for fulfillment and growth. Unintentionally we have planned for servicing the needs of people locked into situations in which substantial growth and reasonable fulfillment are impossible.

2. Cities Are People.   Again, cities are not systems. Cities are people. Our language even presents a problem in regard to conveying this truth. Yet however difficult it may be to reveal the human dimension of our urban setting as fundamental, this must be accomplished, if we are to plan realistically for our continued life and healthy growth. If we can learn from our present urban distress that our cities are people, then perhaps we shall be in a position to apply this lesson to parallel conditions elsewhere in the nation. Our suburban communities as well as our ghettoes suffer in terms of the human condition.

At times I take the Erie-Lackawanna train to work in Newark. On the late evening train back to Orange there have been signs of human misery far more pronounced that one may find on Public Service Bus Number 118, the "Junky Express," which many of the local narcotics addicts ride back and forth between Newark and New York.

On the Erie-Lackawanna train one may see, headed for the nearby and more remote suburbs, bleary-eyed people pacing the aisle unsteadily with partially napkin-covered cans of beer and others drinking their hard liquor mixed or straight. But look into their faces, and one sees grotesque signs of human pain and sadness almost unknown even in the bleak heartlands of our central cities. Home or office, or life in general, would seem too hard to face. There are countless other signs that we need catharsis and redevelopment with respect to our specifically human potential.

Shall we continue to work to renew the physical fabric of our central cities in order that they may be a skewed or compressed copy of our suburban landscapes? Do we honestly believe that cities are brick and mortar, steel and glass, and asphalt and an occasional patch of struggling green? Our suburban environment has more than sufficient human problems; and the difficulties of those whose pain is acute is intensified by the shortcomings of others who feel too inadequate or insecure to face even their near neighbor's distress.

The faulty approach to the nation's power dynamics on the part of the black community is an enlarged image of the destructive approach to power relations that is crippling our homes and communities. The dynamics of existing power relations in our homes (the subject of most of psychiatry) and in our communities (the matter of who really governs) need to be thoughtfully and critically reexamined and reevaluated for the greater good of all. The alternative to planning for continuing creative adjustments is the ceaseless confrontation with capricious change. This can only serve to break our spirit of freedom as our corporate life becomes determined by reactions to forces that are seen to be beyond our power of control.

The failure of black people to come to grips with the matter of their identity reflects one of our most basic national deficiencies. As a nation and as individuals, we who comprise America have not yet discovered exactly who we are.

There have not been significant and continuing signs that our cities see themselves in terms other than white. Black people have not been included in the working identity of our cities. They are the "nonpeople," they are "nonwhite." Small wonder, then, that black people have not been treated as though they should have equity in the city's life. Those we include only incidentally in our corporate image we do not need to consider, except in terms of a needless annoyance, in our planning and work.

Senator Abraham Ribicoff, in the Phi Beta Kappa *Key Reporter*, is reported to have underscored the human aspect of our environment. He stated: "The question Lewis Mumford posed for urban society as a whole applies to America in particular. And that is whether mankind shall devote himself to the development of his own deepest humanity, or whether he shall surrender himself to the now almost automatic forces he has set in motion. . . . The choice is that simple—and that crucial."

3. System and situational changes. We hear so much about economic and technological changes, and their implications for man. Our focus then is directed toward specific changes without our relating them to the systems and situations from which they emerge and to which they give ongoing shape. But the most significant aspect of our current changes is the fact that they will be continuing and accelerating. It is to the continuing and accelerating nature of change itself that we must, then, give primary attention.

So much of our present and past planning has been accomplished on the assumption that we must plan for a new day, and that when the new day comes, all will be well. But that day, as every day thereafter, turns out to be a day of fresh and possibly even greater change. Hence, planning instruments must develop new definitions of order consonant with an enabling of continuing growth and interchange. This task is basic. The alternative to planning for thoughtful and continuing change can only be planning for repression.

The key ingredient in planning for change is continuing public enlightenment. Only as people are aware of the changing requirements of changing times can we even hope to affect the planning that will bring fulfillment and peace to our cities, our nation, and our world.

Without serious planning for change, we compromise those we engage to uphold the public trust. This is precisely what we have done with our policemen who come to their work, we must suppose, with a more than average commitment to facilitate the public peace. Yet because we have not come to terms with the need for all in our society to have a sense of equity and investment, our policing agents are placed unwittingly in positions of catalysts and scapegoats in our present urban strife.

Our whole view of life—and of our institutions—must be altered to accommodate the changes that are inevitable, whether planned or unplanned. A society that overlooks reality is by definition psychotic. Those who build the most complete fairylands are to be found in our mental institutions.

Much of the reaction to our current unrest has a psychotic flavor. It closes its mind to the tardiness of change, and to its inevitability and legitimacy. Policemen who are informed by a society that is itself informed will be reasonably expected to be among the best resources for good in our cities. Our teachers and other public servants will also be far greater assets than we might presently imagine. That our society is not informed in ways that a changing world decrees is evident in the educational statistics for every city in the nation. We still speak of the need for a high school diploma. What is needed is continuing education, in vocational and avocational pursuits, for everyone in our society from the cradle to the grave. Plato, in *The Republic* (Book VI), speaks of the irony even in his day of relatively little change, of educating the young and giving little education to the older persons who must make informed and wise decisions.

4. Self-interest. People are most highly motivated in those concerns where their own welfare is critically at stake. Any planning for our cities that does not clearly reveal the life-and-death nature of the present situation will be neither effective nor responsible.

A leading figure in this nation, who has observed the caustic ferment in our inner cities, recently wrote:

As I have rubbed elbows with those who live in the ghetto, as I have listened to the voice of revolt, I am more convinced than ever before that *unless we reverse our course* [italics mine], build a new America, the old America will be destroyed.

Time is running out for those who have responsibilities for the tranquility of the nation. The seeds of revolution have been sown. They cannot be rooted out by force.

While we must maintain law and order, we must either achieve orderly progress or change will be inflicted with mortal wounds. Either we shall join hands, hearts, and minds and march together on paths of fulfillment for all, or we shall find ourselves torn asunder.[2]

The spirit of Governor Romney's words must be structured into our planning instruments designed for the nation's survival.

Self-interest can never be served when we commit our resources to the wrong problems. Canon Dielard Robinson of Trinity Cathedral in Newark, in noting the tragically oversimplified view the Essex County clergy were apparently taking of Newark's postrebellion situation, commented. "Those who praise the Lord, and pass the wrong ammunition, are in serious trouble, indeed."

[2] The *New York Times*, October 1, 1967.

6 Self-Defeating Goals

As we have pointed out, the cities have had far more than their fair share of problems to face from burdens rightfully belonging to the suburbs and to the nation at large. Seriously compounding these gross unplanned inequities has been the failure to make a sufficient critical reassessment of three specific goals we have assumed to be appropriate. The three goals are expressed in the terms equality, integration, and order. Contrary to our best hopes or intentions, much of the manner in which we have sought to apply these goals has been self-defeating and has added in a tragically ironic way to the increasing unrest in our cities.

EQUALITY AS A GOAL

Until the present, America has never had to put to the test the national goal of equality of opportunity. In the past, the presence of the frontier of undeveloped and largely free resources and the nature of our mixed farm and factory economy gave opportunity to those sufficiently self-directing to seek it. The open frontier of the past no longer remains and our economy is no longer wide open at the bottom. Opportunity today exists almost solely for those who have both initiative and hope. Even so, for those who belong to groups that represent low status and lack of power, such opportunities are greatly proscribed. The proscription of opportunity applies from the higher echelons of insurance and banking to certain religious and nationality groups. It was the surprising experience of the Massachusetts Commission against Discrimination in its early days that a large portion of complaints of discrimination were received from persons belonging to particular religious and foreign nationality groups.

Equality of opportunity is not a fact, in spite of our massive commitments. It may be that "equality" per se is an impossible goal, and as such can only serve to frustrate the social and economic problems of our cities to a greater degree.

The term itself has several built-in difficulties. The simple affirmation of equality with others as a personal goal involves an implicit acceptance or declaration of one's own inferiority. If one's goal is to be equal, one must at present be less than equal. For one to affirm one's inferiority is, in and of itself, the imposition of a liability. This is particularly true of black people in America who have not been permitted, by any large-scale means, to affirm their inherent sense of dignity and worth. Black self-hate and hopelessness provide the context in which the goal of "equality" is projected. Under such explicit circumstances, the goal of equality with white America creates its own self-limiting apparatus.

THE NEED FOR EQUITY

Again, the goal of equality has a static element about it. It does not invest others with a willingness to share effectively in creating the new relationship of equality. It's as though one wished to enter a family circle in which continuing relationships had already been built. If those within the circle do not make significant adjustments in their previous and present relationships, the one who seeks to enter will remain an "outsider" forever. We all know of many such circumstances in our own experience.

Robert Curvin, Director of the Rutgers University Community Action Training Center, provided much of the leadership for prerebellion protests in the City of Newark. He indicates that the absence of a disposition toward equitable treatment for black people in New Jersey has resulted in constant frustration. In a report on the Tri-City Community Organization for Development Mr. Curvin writes:

According to the 1960 census, there are 527,000 non-whites in New Jersey of a total population of 6,066,000. However, the interests of the block of black people are continually ignored or defeated. It is interesting to analyze the outcome of status of a few issues that recently stirred excitement in the black community of New Jersey, and especially in the City of Newark.

See Table XIII.

TABLE XIII   Outcome of Issues Relating to Black People in New Jersey

ISSUE	PREFERENCE OF BLACK COMMUNITY	OUTCOME OR STATUS
Broad-base tax	Graduated income tax	Sales tax
Reapportionment	Senatorial Elections by Subdistrict	Elections at large
Welfare	Passage of ADC-UP	No action
Bussing	Against use of government funds for parochial school bussing	Passage of bill allowing use of government funds for bussing parochial school students
Cabinet appointments	Appointment of qualified black person as Commissioner of Education	Appointment of white person

Mr. Curvin adds the comment: "In each local community throughout New Jersey this pattern of defeat is duplicated and often with immediate damaging consequences. Even in the city of Newark, where black people represent 52% of the total population, they are pitifully represented."

One who wishes to enter into an already formed circle does not seek equality with those already present. Rather he hopes to have some reasonable equity in the new circle of relationships. When the goal is equity, the newcomer's presence can be seen as widening the circle and enriching its possibilities. Those within will know adjustment will be called for, and that such adjustment will work to the potential benefit of all. Equity has about it a dynamic and motivating edge that is missing from the term equality. Hence, people may commit themselves to equality and not be inspired to make the change of pace, of outlook or of plans that would make equality possible.

Such has been the case, to some degree, in our cities, where protestations of sincerity concerning the unchanging plight of black people have resulted in the continuation of conditions as they are. In the Newark Public Schools, in the police and fire departments, and in the administrative offices and boards of the City of Newark the relative low status of black people has remained unchanged. Indeed, in the light of the vastly increased population proportions of black people in Newark, the relative influence of black people in city government has decreased over a period of twenty years.

Equity for all would mean, as the term implies, an enlargement in our conception of fair play. It would mean that everyone in the nation is included—according to his abilities and needs—in the responsibilities and benefit levels of our local, state, and national life. This is, after all, the goal we seek to attain in our homes when others are added to the family circle. Where any member of the family is not given equity, problems and pain for the family as a whole result.

St. Thomas More, in Book II, Chapter I, of his *Utopia*, wrote of the ideal city as one in which each looks to the needs of all. "Political justice," wrote Aristotle, "is manifested between persons who share a common way of life which has for its object a state of affairs in which they will have all that they need for an *independent existence* as free and *proportionally* members of the society. Between persons who do not enjoy such freedom and proportionality there can be no political justice but only a simulacrum of it." (*Ethics*, Book V, Chapter 6. Italics mine.)

Aristotle wrote further of the place of equity in public life:

Equity, though a higher thing than one form of justice, is itself just and is not geometrically different from justice. Thus, so far as both are good, they coincide, though equity is to be preferred. What puzzles people is that equity is not the justice of the law courts but a method of restoring the balance of justice when it has been tilted by the law. We see now what equity is, and that it is just and superior to one kind of justice. And this lets us also see clearly the nature of the equitable man. He is one who by deliberate choice has taught himself the habit of doing equitable things, who is not a stickler for his rights to the disadvantage of others but refrains from pressing his claims even when he has the law on his side. It is a disposition of this kind which finds its expression in equity—equity which we have just shown to be a species of justice and not a disposition of a different genus altogether. [*Ethics*, Book V, Chapter 10.]

Plato disparages the goal of equality by speaking of "equality of a sort, distributed to equal and unequal alike." (*The Republic,* Book VIII.)

THE NEED FOR EXCELLENCE

Returning from Washington, D.C., in late August 1967, from the initial meeting of the Urban Coalition, I boarded an airplane in the company of two "black brothers" who had attended the July 20–23 National Conference on Black Power. As I approached a seat where two of us could be together, a voice cried out, "Let me sit there," and added, "You are Dr. Nathan Wright, aren't you?" "I am Nathan Wright," I answered. Then the man asked my companions, "Please, let me sit next to Dr. Wright. It is very important." My companions agreed to seek seats elsewhere. My new companion explained to me that he was Jewish and that he had wanted desperately to be in touch with me to share what he considered a crucial insight. "We Jews," he said, "have never sought equality. That is degrading on its face. We have always sought excellence; and no one may quarrel with that. Black people have so much critical insight and so many other unused gifts for us all to benefit from. But black people cannot give of themselves as they must do, if they are not encouraged to excel."

Equity and excellence. These are the two goals in place of

TABLE "A" [XIV] Summary Table of School Medians Based Upon the Stanford Reading Test, Intermediate, Form K, and the Kuhlmann-Anderson Intelligence Test, Form F

GRADE 6

SCHOOL CODE NO.	C.A.	IQ[1]	M.A.	TOTAL AVERAGE READING AGE EQUIV- ALENT	READING GRADE EQUIVALENTS		
					PARA- GRAPH MEAN- ING	WORD MEAN- ING	TOTAL AVERAGE
1	11–5	92	10–7	9–7	4.3	4.6	4.5
2	11–5	93	10–8	9–7	4.4	4.6	4.5
3	11–3	100	11–3	10–1	4.6	5.2	4.9
4	11–3	101	11–6	10–6	4.8	5.7	5.3
5	11–6	93	10–11	10–0	4.6	5.1	4.9
6	11–4	95	10–11	9–5	4.1	4.5	4.3
7	11–4	98	10–11	9–9	4.3	4.9	4.6
8	11–1	112	12–6	11–10	6.3	6.8	6.6
9	11–5	92	10–5	9–6	4.4	4.4	4.4
10	11–5	92	10–7	9–4	4.2	4.3	4.3
11	11–4	90	10–4	9–2	3.9	4.2	4.1
12	11–3	101	11–4	9–11	4.6	5.0	4.8
13	11–1	106	11–8	11–2	5.4	6.4	5.9
15	11–3	96	10–9	9–8	4.3	4.8	4.6
16	11–2	100	11–3	10–4	4.9	5.3	5.1
17	11–1	101	11–4	10–4	4.5	5.9	5.2
18	11–3	97	11–0	9–11	4.6	5.0	4.8
19	11–2	108	11–11	11–9	6.3	6.6	6.5
21	11–2	102	11–5	10–2	4.8	5.2	5.0
22	11–5	94	10–7	9–5	4.2	4.5	4.4
23	11–2	105	11–11	10–11	5.1	6.2	5.7
24	11–3	103	11–8	10–8	5.0	5.9	5.5
26	11–5	93	10–6	9–5	4.3	4.4	4.4
29	11–4	94	10–10	9–8	4.4	4.7	4.6
30	11–4	89	10–1	9–2	4.1	4.1	4.1
31	11–3	95	10–10	9–8	4.3	4.8	4.6
33	11–1	117	12–10	11–11	6.1	7.1	6.6
34	11–5	92	10–7	9–4	4.2	4.3	4.3
35	11–6	91	10–5	9–3	4.0	4.2	4.1
36	11–2	104	11–7	11–2	5.2	6.6	5.9
37	11–4	95	10–9	9–8	4.5	4.6	4.6
38	11–6	97	11–3	10–5	4.9	5.4	5.2
39	11–3	95	10–6	9–5	4.3	4.2	4.3

TABLE "A" [XIV]—(*Continued*)

SCHOOL CODE NO.	C.A.	IQ[1]	M.A.	TOTAL AVERAGE READING AGE EQUIVALENT	READING GRADE EQUIVALENTS		
					PARA- GRAPH MEAN- ING	WORD MEAN- ING	TOTAL AVERAGE
40	11–4	93	10–7	9–4	4.1	4.4	4.3
41	11–4	100	11–5	10–1	4.8	5.1	5.0
42	11–5	99	11–4	10–4	4.9	5.3	5.1
43	11–4	99	11–3	10–1	4.7	5.1	4.9
44	11–6	90	10–6	9–3	4.0	4.3	4.2
45	11–6	92	10–6	9–4	4.1	4.3	4.2
46	11–6	93	10–11	9–6	4.2	4.7	4.5
47	11–4	98	11–3	10–4	4.8	5.4	5.1
48	11–1	112	12–6	12–2	6.4	7.3	6.9
49	11–4	99	11–2	9–11	4.5	5.1	4.8
50	11–4	95	10–9	9–9	4.4	4.9	4.7
53	11–2	113	12–7	12–5	6.4	7.7	7.1
55	11–5	93	10–8	9–9	4.3	4.9	4.6
City	11–5	97	11–0	9–10	4.5	4.9	4.7

[1] IQ medians are computed from school distributions and not from median ages.

equality toward which we should encourage everyone in every circumstance throughout the nation.

Nowhere are the goals of equity and excellence for all more urgently needed than in our educational enterprise, especially as it exists in our cities. The sum total of deaths from all the wars we have fought in this present century do not approach the number of casualties resulting from our entirely unintended failures in education.

In the City of Newark, the average black student in 1963 was 1.5 years below national standards in reading. The then Acting Director of the Newark Human Rights Commission explained:

Taking the sixth grade level as our medium, this means that thousands of Negro youths are still reading at a third and fourth grade level, but are in sixth grade due to so-called "social promotions." This can only lead to an inadequately prepared adult, most likely, one who has joined the increasing ranks of school drop-outs.

This causes THE MOST SERIOUS PROBLEM IN NEWARK TODAY. It is from these aimless, hopeless, and helpless youths, in whom the spark of frustration exists, that the fire which kindles race riots can be found.

Physical facilities, no matter how new or modern, do not compensate for a teaching staff which is, by virtue of its high turnover and liberal use of substitute teachers, inadequate to the task of educating in an area where in-home encouragement is relatively lacking for learning situations. Table A [XIV] and B [XV] are statistics based on the Board of Education's city wide testing program for October, 1963. A close look at the statistics will indicate that the city's grade six reading level for "paragraph meaning" is grade 4.5, that "word meaning" for grade six is 4.9 and total average is grade 4.7. This is significant because there are five city schools where the reading grade equivalents are above the national average.[1]

The basic story told here may be repeated in terms of all our cities. Even in St. Louis, where Dr. Samuel Sheppard, one of the ablest public schoolmen in the land, has made such a notable effort at human reclamation, success for our urban schools is still remote. Indeed, as Boston's Bryant Rollins points out, even at the present rate of accelerated educational improvement and innovation it may take as long as seventy years for black youth in our urban schools to catch up with their white brothers.

EDUCATIONAL ADJUSTMENTS

If excellence and equity are to be our national goals in place of equality, then several major adjustments must be made not only in our urban schools, but also in our schools outside the city.

1. Perspective. My own educational experience as a black youth was somewhat different from the average. My mother was a school teacher and my grandmother, who cared for the household, was a former school teacher. My father was college trained, and possessed a literary and poetic skill which neither my slightly older sisters nor my brother and I have been able to equal.

Perhaps most telling in my educational experience was my attendance in Cincinnati at the Walnut Hills High School, a Latin School in the tradition of the Boston Latin School. Walnut Hills High School was entered by competition. All four of the children in our family went there.

[1] *Human Relations Profile*, Newark, 1965.

TABLE "B" [XV]) Summary Table of School Medians Based Upon the Stanford Arithmetic Test, Intermediate, Form Km

GRADE 7

SCHOOL CODE NO.	REASONING		COMPUTATION		TOTAL ARITHMETIC AVG.	
	GRADE	AGE	GRADE	AGE	GRADE	AGE
3	5.3	10–6	5.7	11–0	5.5	10–9
5	6.3	11–5	6.3	11–6	6.3	11–6
6	5.1	10–3	5.4	10–8	5.3	10–6
7	5.3	10–6	5.6	10–11	5.5	10–9
9	4.7	9–10	5.2	10–5	5.0	10–2
11	4.8	10–0	5.3	10–7	5.1	10–4
12	5.4	10–7	5.7	11–0	5.6	10–10
13	6.7	11–10	7.4	12–9	7.1	12–4
15	4.8	10–0	5.6	10–11	5.2	10–6
17	6.0	11–3	6.9	12–3	6.5	11–9
18	6.8	12–0	7.2	12–7	7.0	12–4
21	6.1	11–3	7.1	12–5	6.6	11–10
23	7.0	12–3	7.3	12–8	7.2	12–6
24	6.6	11–9	7.7	13–0	7.2	12–5
26	4.4	9–6	4.3	9–6	4.4	9–6
30	4.7	9–10	4.8	10–1	4.8	10–0
31	5.1	10–3	5.4	10–8	5.3	10–6
33	8.5	14–0	8.2	13–7	8.4	13–10
36	7.0	12–3	7.3	12–8	7.2	12–6
37	4.8	10–0	5.4	10–8	5.1	10–4
38	5.1	10–3	5.5	10–9	5.3	10–6
40	4.6	9–9	4.4	9–7	4.5	9–8
41	6.0	11–3	6.2	11–6	6.1	11–5
42	5.9	11–2	6.3	11–6	6.1	11–4
45	4.9	10–1	4.6	9–10	4.8	10–0
46	5.7	10–11	6.1	11–5	5.9	11–2
47	6.0	11–3	6.4	11–8	6.2	11–6
48	7.7	13–0	7.6	12–11	7.7	13–0
49	5.3	10–6	6.1	11–5	5.7	11–0
50	5.4	10–7	5.9	11–3	5.7	10–11
51	4.8	10–0	4.5	9–9	4.7	9–11
52	5.4	10–7	5.9	11–3	5.7	10–11
53	7.2	12–6	7.0	12–4	7.1	12–5
54	5.7	10–11	5.9	11–3	5.8	11–1
55	5.0	10–2	4.8	10–1	4.9	10–2
City	5.3	10–6	5.6	10–11	5.5	10–9

(The five schools participating in the Newark Plan are included in this table with their scores on the Metropolitan Arithmetic Test, Intermediate. AM, converted to Stanford Arithmetic Test, Intermediate, KM, grade and age equivalents.)

Walnut Hills, was, and still is, a prestigious school. In the 1930's and 1940's the well-to-do in Cincinnati still sent their children to the public schools. Sons and daughters of patricians sought to enter Walnut Hills; the atmosphere of the school was aristocratic. Teachers taught students in whom they saw the best potential. The students felt a sense of purpose and determination. The teachers, perhaps most notably, imparted a view of life that had about it a majestic air. The students were taught to believe that they were called to live, learn, and serve majestically in a world worthy of those who might be kings.

Our education at Walnut Hills High School provided us each day with a sample of what life might yet be. It was a pleasant, immediately rewarding, horizon-widening, and growth-producing experience. Students spend more of their waking hours at the business of school than at any other activity. Surely this activity should invest life for every pupil with a sense of its actual and potential glory.

The basic task to which our schools should be committed is the glorification of human life. A disposition toward excellence, according to each child's own unique potential, would result from such a process.

2. Self-awareness. A pupil learns largely by role identification. One sees himself as a doctor or as a scientist. The pupil learns each day in relation to that future role. If pupils have no hope for the future and are not self-aware, there are no frameworks upon which to place the building blocks of each day's schooling.

People communicate best by being self-aware. People who are not self-aware have difficulty in communicating with others. This is true largely for two reasons. We may confuse our feelings with the feelings or the needs of others. We may block out of our vision of reality those whose presence is threatening because they remind us too much of realities from which we would escape.

Thus in our urban schools the matter of self-awareness presents potential problems on the part of both the teachers and the taught. Teachers in our urban schools come in ever-larger numbers from teacher training colleges. Suburban schools have a proportionately large number of teachers from liberal arts institutions. Those who teach in our urban schools should be made particularly aware of the potential problems and advantages afforded by their own educational and socioeconomic background with respect to their urban teaching tasks. Far too little has been done in this regard. A teacher who is not aware of the daily and hour-by-hour influence of his or her cultural perceptions creates loss rather than gain in our schools and our society.

Teachers should make their craft into a profession by requiring of themselves, as basic, the master's degree. This would build a stronger self-image for the profession. It would also allow for far more time to be devoted to the human relations skills essential to relating to others we would encourage to excel.

For pupils, self-awareness disciplines should be provided. If an hour of group therapy were provided weekly for all pupils every third year, I.Q.'s would tend to go up and disciplinary problems would be greatly reduced. The cost would be minimal. People who are self-aware have an enlarged capacity to be purposeful and creative in what they do.

In an examination of pupil essays in one project associated with a major public school system, the following was reported:

> The personality of the teacher is a dominant influence in a child's life. Essays written in classrooms led by an obviously warm, encouraging and understanding teacher abound in lively detail and inner riches even if the children's intellectual potential is rather on the low side. Essays written under guidance of domineering, distant, perhaps rejecting teachers are dry and void of any personality-revealing content. The children stultified, regardless of intellectual endowment.
>
> Outstanding among early childhood events related by the writers is the frequency of moving. Children not older than 12 years may have moved as often as 6 times and attended 4–6 different schools. All those who are ready to relate feelings connected with facts deplore this mobility. A direct result is the high frequency of planning for a house of one's own, where children can grow up undisturbed, expressed in the "biographies of the future." The need for strengthening both the children's self-reliance and their ability to become vocationally and financially fit to establish themselves as members of a stable society is obvious.
>
> Tabulation of the children's vocational choices show a deplorable absence of information as to a changing culture and the many types of work available today. The most frequently mentioned future vocations are, in this order: teacher, nurse, secretary, ballplayer. Many

children state merely that they want to have "a job." Adequate vocational guidance and information concerning available high education and ways to prepare for it is one of the major needs in all schools.

Clearly there is a long way to go in the direction of providing our pupils with a larger vision of our world and of their potentially secure and highly prized place within it.

3. Human Development.   No pupil should fail or receive "social promotions" in our schools. Our purpose must be to teach our students and not primarily to test and advise them onto the next step toward the oblivion of no hope

I have taught at the elementary, secondary, and college levels. Most recently I have been teaching at night in a community college that is a part of the University of the City of New York. In my classes at the New York City Community College I have a wide variety of students. There are bright eighteen-year-old young people; there are grandparents who have put their children or grandchildren through graduate schools; there are foreign-born persons experiencing language difficulties; there are persons who have entered by high school equivalency diplomas; and there are teachers preparing for the doctorate. Obviously this presents a situation of greatly mixed needs. Yet I assume that my purpose is primarily to teach them all, not simply to test them.

Therefore, all my students share in formulating suggested examination questions that might test their ability to bring the materials studied into meaningful focus. The questions are critiqued in class and the best are designated. If students learn how to prepare adequate examination questions, they have gained a knowledge of how to organize their materials for study. Then, too, there is no mystery as to what the examination of the course is all about. What if a student fails? He is assigned additional work that is simple and designed to help him master what he has missed. When this work is completed satisfactorily, the mark is adjusted upward. Learning is basic; the testing is only a part of the process.

Term papers are due by mid-semester. I read them and offer my own criticisms, in the light of which the students may re-do them and receive—always—a highly satisfactory mark. In life situations we are not given marks. If a task is not done well, we do it over until it is right. Students should never be merely left with "C" or

"B" marks. They should be encouraged and helped toward the greatest proficiency in the tasks of self-criticism and self-improvement. This is not social promotion. It is the encouragement of self-directed growth into self-sufficiency.

4. **Aggressive Determination.** I refer to the commitment of our best resources to the nation's most urgent task, that of human resource development. A look at expenditures per pupil and pupil drop-out rates, especially at the two high schools of greatest black pupil concentration in Newark, should shed some light upon both the need for determination and the self-defeating nature of "equal" opportunity in our city schools.

Such had been the process of in-migration and containment that by 1960, 63 percent of the black population of Newark lived in the two areas of the city served by Central High School and South Side High. There were 91,000 black people living in these two school districts. The population in both of these districts was 72 percent black, 28 percent white. The total population was 128,486.

The average family income in the Central High School District in 1960 was $3,185.88. The median number of school years completed by adults twenty-five years old or over was 8.4 years. In all but one of the sixteen census tracts within the district, the average family income was under $4,000. In two of the census tract areas the median number of school years completed was less than eight years.

The South Side High School District can be described in identical terms with respect to racial characteristics. However, it appears that more of the black population breaking out of the constraints of poverty, but confined to the housing ghetto, resided in this district. The average family income for the district was $3,962.00 There is a full $796 or 24.9 percent above the average family income in the Central High District. The number of school years completed by those twenty-five years of age or over was 8.9. Again, this was somewhat higher than the 8.4 median years of schooling for the Central High District. Finally, there were four census tracts of the 13 in the district in which average family income was about $4,000. There was no census tract in the district with a median number of less than 8 school years completed.

In Table XVI below we see the per pupil expenditures, in the

1965 account, over a five-year period for each of the city's high schools.

In 1960 the average per pupil expenditure citywide was $554. Four years later the city was spending an average of $528 per pupil. It was actually spending less per pupil in 1964–65 than it did in 1960–61. This serves to illustrate the growing problem of finding funds to meet increasing enrollments. However, of more interest at this point is where those funds were being spent.

TABLE XVI   Per Pupil Expenditures

SCHOOL	1960–61	1961–62	1962–63	1963–64	1964–65	AVERAGE
Arts High	$600	$635	$569	$590	$613	$601
Barringer	552	594	531	489	594	552
Central	614	700	537	471	492	562
East Side	503	513	491	468	509	496
South Side	593	583	574	516	552	563
Vailsburg	—	—	588	543	521	550
Weequahic	495	495	498	488	466	488
West Side	605	630	566	493	535	565
Total	544	573	535	493	528	536

Central High School, with the highest percentage of students dropping out of school, received in 1964–65 less than the average per pupil allocation. South Side High School, with the second highest percentage of students dropping out of school, received the third highest per pupil allocation. Arts High School, with the lowest percentage of students dropping out of school, received the highest per pupil allocation. See Table XVII.

The greatest resources should always go where there is the greatest need. This is true in our families; it must be true in our cities and throughout the nation if we are to preserve and develop our human capital.

Pupils in our schools must not be looked upon as statistics. They represent the substance of America. As long as one potential drop-out remains poorly developed and is not fully encouraged toward growth into his or her best self, just so long have we failed through our schools. There is no "law of averages" for success in

TABLE XVII Cumulative Dropout Rates for Graduating Class of 1965

SCHOOL	NUMBER OF GRADUATES	DROPOUTS 4th YEAR HIGH SCHOOL		1ST YEAR COLLEGE		2D YEAR COLLEGE		TOTAL	
		NO.	PERCENT	NO.	PERCENT	NO.	PERCENT	NO.	PERCENT
Central	344	310	47.4%	56	16%	23	7%	79	23%
South Side	325	310	47.4	56	16	23	7	143	44
West Side	405	158	28.1	115	28	56	14	171	42
Weequahic	506	76	13.1	257	51	62	12	319	63
Barringer	508	95	13.8	181	36	37	7	218	43
East Side	443	189	29.9	93	21	30	7	123	28
Vailsburg	265	51	16.1	123	46	21	8	144	54
Arts High	143	19	11.7	91	64	14	9	105	73

promoting human growth. Education must come to be seen as an "all or nothing task."

INTEGRATION AS A GOAL

Like the term "equality," "integration" should also be subjected to critical scrutiny. That it has caused endless acrimony is certain. All social goals must be expressed in terms of ends, not means. Integration should have been looked upon as a means toward the end of "freedom." So it has been with the legal integration of the English and the Irish, and of the Germans and the Jews. Enforced integration of these and practically all other major ethnic groups has been achieved unself-consciously as a part of a larger purpose. It was assumed to be basic to the provision of the greatest freedom of choice, consonant with the preservation of the rights and integrity of others. Effectively what other ethnic groups have enjoyed is a kind of desegregation, where in private matters the maximum of free choice has been preserved and in public matters the public interest of our citizens has been uppermost.

Full desegregation for black people would have meant more enforced integration than we have experienced thus far, but only as a means toward approaching freedom. Integration, according to the manner in which it has been expressed in our schools, has not meant freedom. Unintentionally it has revealed itself in terms of manipulation. To change or enforce school boundaries on a rational basis may make for freedom, but the artificial moving of children about so that one group's presence in particular might benefit the other is both denigrating and manipulative. When black children are in the presence of upper-class white children in school, they are in the presence of children who, unlike themselves, have a deep sense of hope and self-awareness.

The mind-set of manipulation is far too prevalent in the nation's life. To some degree it lies behind the ideological conflict between our two major political parties. It lies behind much of the tension caused, among white liberals in particular, over the impetus toward self-directed black efforts into self-sufficiency and self-respect. It was a manipulative mind-set that sought to force a medical-dental college in Newark.

If lower-class white children were put in the presence of self-directed and hopeful black children, the lower-class white children would tend to learn better. What is needed is not arbitrary bussing but the development of the self awareness and hope that bussing, under some circumstances, creates.

The turn toward bussing must be understood in part against a background of utter frustration in our urban schools. These schools were failing to do their task, and they were becoming segregated. The two must go together causally. Hence, we desegregate as an answer.

Depending on the circumstances, black children may learn even better with other black children. Black people need a basic sense of pride in their own indelibly permanent blackness, but it is clearly un-American for persons to be arbitrarily segregated by any of the many forms of sophistry used to limit freedom of opportunity for black people.

It may well be better for different kinds of pupils to know each other and to learn how to live together. If "knowing each other" is our purpose, then we should advertise it as such and not as "integration." Integration, except in an intimate social sense, should be seen only as a means to a denigrating and manipulative end. Desegregation is a larger concept, assuming the conditions whereby social integration might take place as a part of a process creating maximum freedom while insuring the integrity of everyone.

During February 1967, at the height of the medical-dental school controversy, the Center for Research in Marketing, Inc., in Peekskill, New York, conducted a survey to determine the attitudes of the twenty-two thousand black residents of the area to be cleared. The conclusion of the report reads in part:

> The study indicates that the population of the affected area is not adequately informed as to the facts regarding the building of the proposed medical-dental school. Although about two-thirds of the population have heard something about the proposal, the vast majority are not aware of its purpose, its location, its immediacy, or their rights.
>
> On the other hand, the population appears to be resigned to the necessity of doing what it is told to do. There is little active resistance to the necessity of uprooting oneself. However, there is a high degree of skepticism and cynicism concerning the reasons for building the new facility, and the degree to which it will provide improved medical and dental care for Negroes.
>
> This is not to say that our respondents do not see themselves

faced by a myriad of uncomfortable and unhappy problems. They talk of the dislocation of the children and their education. They worry about the rental costs of the new apartment and the cost of moving, and transportation to their jobs from a new location. They suspect that the purpose of choosing this location is to disenfranchise the Negro in Newark . . .

Certainly the officialdom of the city appears to have done little to fulfill its function of creating an informed populace in the affected area. The survey conducted by some official body was for some of our respondents the first inkling they had of the imminent destruction of their homes. The cruel and thoughtless form of the questionnaire did not really serve to inform but rather to frighten.

The crassly manipulative mind-set evident here may also be seen in the demand, by the teacher's union in Newark, to give operation Head Start job preferences to the predominantly white staff of the schools. The simple economic aspect of black poverty would seem to suggest, however, that all economic returns from tackling black poverty be given, wherever possible, to black people. Further, the black youth in Head Start need the presence of the greater image of black success. It is ironic to say the least that in the very efforts designed to end black poverty we aggravate and extend it. This is no less than a continuing of the long-standing financial exploitation of black people.

Controversy over total integration had added untold woes to the already heavy burdens of our cities. Several things should be clear about it.

1. The term itself implies deliberate mixing (that is, manipulation). Desegregation, which seems preferable as a term, suggests a total clearing of the slate for the maximum of choice, consistent with the rights of all. Is this not what we want?

2. Integration has come to imply a sense of evil in ethnic self-awareness. Yet ethnocentrism is the most universal of social traits. False views of the almost absolute good of integration have encouraged black self-hate. We cannot afford to be dogmatic in any theoretically based concern. All social ideas must be looked upon as tentative and be subjected to a continuing exposure to light.

3. The desegregation (which may be preferable) or the integration of staff, that is, its deliberate mixing, is a proper function

of the schools and other agencies. Staff is "under orders" and should be sent wherever it can be most effective. The across the board bussing of students, like the integration of church congregations, may be in large measure an unconscious dodge that masks the more realistic, and far simpler task of staff desegregation.

4. The choice of the term integration may also reflect our hesitancy to accept the fact that black people, as black people, have suffered at the hands of our society, including their own, for too long. Black people's problems are not unique, but are the problems of others *in extremis*. Instead of focusing upon scattering the "problem cases," it should seem advantageous to focus upon them in whatever is the most direct and honest way.

5. An inherent limitation of both integration in this sense and desegration is the failure of either term to suggest the need for a closing of the gap between white and black Americans.

We must define our terms in relation to American needs, and although "desegregation" has its limitations, it would seem to be the only means of eliminating a large measure of current confusion. And with regard to educational opportunity, there absolutely needs to be an integration of a far different kind than we have considered as seriously as we should.

INTEGRATION OF ADULTS IN LEARNING

Our society shortchanges itself by not saturating its adult environment with the atmosphere of learning. New Jersey State Education Commissioner, Carl L. Marburger, in mid-September 1967, stated that the pace of change in American society has been so rapid that it will be possible for a person's skills to become obsolete four times in his life. Some economists predict even greater changes, but Mr. Marburger added: "All vocational education must gear itself for constant change and flexibility and account for this in any plans for the future . . . we need further research and development for proper guidance as well as *improved occupational requirement forecasting*." (Italics mine.)[2] Education, as we noted earlier, has tended the furnaces of industry and is

[2] *Newark Star Ledger*, September 23, 1967.

geared to serve primarily the needs of other institutions rather than the fundamental purpose of human growth.

If people must be continually trained and retrained in the years ahead, then we must somehow get away from the notion that education is chiefly for youth. Education must become a continuing human process. If that is to be so, then we should seek to ascertain just what kinds of new educational instruments may be most appropriate and efficient for our radically new needs. The kind of educational enterprise we have assumed to be appropriate for young people in the past may not be appropriate for adult continuing educational needs in the future. Several propositions need to be borne in mind.

1. **Motivation.**   One of our major problems with adult education is lack of motivation. Those who are not self-directed need continuing adult education most. Our typical middle-class methods of motivation convey contempt to the hopeless youth and adults in our cities. There is also increasing evidence that the same results are being obtained among suburban youth. As a result, our motivational devices must be reexamined.

Commissioner Marburger warned in mid-September 1967 that the state of New Jersey is in a "deadly race against the time bomb of angry and uneducated youth. . . . These are the youths who demonstrate their frustration looting and burning . . . young men and women with nowhere to go because they don't have the skills to take them." We should let the symptoms of strife in our cities be a clear reminder of far more extensive needs in our society. These restless youths will become the bewildered and infuriated adults of tomorrow.

2. **Status.**   As cities throughout the nation do, Newark provides Adult Basic Education. This helps with a few adults, but not too many. For an adult to seek "basic" education is denigrating. People must be challenged to move ahead, to work toward fulfillment, not to "come up to standard."

In my recent book, *Black Power and Urban Unrest: Creative Possibilities,* I set forth some basic elements required for planning for status and other motivational needs of continuing adult education for all. My next book, *Programs for Power: New Approaches to Urban Regeneration,* will contain a detailed model, together with a critique, of an institution for continuing adult education in the kind of world that lies ahead. The urgency of our developing new approaches lies in the fact that all who vote—whether at the polls, at the welfare office, in our jails, or by poisoning the reservoirs of our towns, suburbs and cities—must be encouraged to develop some more adequate conception of life and their potential place in it. Those who see education as one more means of denying their human dignity will not turn to it freely, either for their own good or for the good of the nation.

3. Facilities.   Facilities are already available for integrating our adults into our ongoing education enterprise. The greatest single waste of the taxpayers' resources is represented by our unused school facilities, at night and during the summer vacation period.

It is a strange commentary on our educational process that an adult with little formal education may get a high school equivalency certificate in less than twelve months' time. Some far more than superficial adjustments are certainly called for in the reordering of our total curriculum if the equivalent of most of twelve years of education may be secured in a year or less.

There is no good reason for any schools to be closed for two to three months of each year. We may rationalize the wisdom for today of a calendar devised a hundred years ago to satisfy the needs of farmers, but the fact remains that education wastes the public resources by not using the total time it has available and by not making the fullest use of public facilities. Where children study twelve months by day, adults may study twelve months by night. Learning is as important as working. We work full-time. Why not learn full-time as well?

The integration of adults into the educational process is basic to the economic needs and public safety of the nation in the days that lie ahead. Plato, writing in a far different age, gives a universal warning that applies to us as we seek civil peace and fulfillment in our cities. He writes of the need for continuing education for adults in a free society. His subject is "how a city shall deal with philosophy so as not to be destroyed itself." He writes of the men of his day:

While they are boys and lads they should occupy themselves with boyish education and philosophy, and train their bodies very carefully while these are growing and coming into manhood; the lads are gaining possession of their bodies as a help to liberal education. Then as their age goes on, the time when the soul begins to be perfected, they should tune up the exercises of the soul; and when decreasing strength puts them outside politics and warfare, from then on let them pasture at will in the meadows, and practise nothing other than philosophy except as a bye-end; those, I mean, who intend to live happily, and when they come to their latter end to crown the life they have led with a fitting portion in the next world.

As we grow in age, we should grow in knowledge and understanding.

A thoughtful reassessment of goals is needed for the cities and the nation. Indeed, in the place of our Commissions on Civil Disorders, those responsible for the public peace might have proposed the creation of bodies for new and far more basic approaches to the ongoing reassessment and implementation of national and local goals.

7 The Perilous Choice: Order or Repression?

"Violence is as American as apple pie," so H. Rap Brown has said. Violence pervades the life of the nation, but it is the symbolic violence, even more than the dramatic overt expressions of violence, that is most corrosive. It is this kind of violence that inflicts its injuries upon the lives of all.

THE NEED FOR ORDERLY CHANGE

To live without the possibility of violence is not to live at all; for life at best is precarious. But at every point in our personal and public life we must be deeply sensitive to the presence and needs of others. This means that we must work for the inclusion and fulfillment of everyone in our society and basic to the continuing inclusion of others is a redefinition of what we mean by "order" within orderly change.

In this light we must understand—although not necessarily agree with—the position of those who react to civic rebellion with the threat of further, but official, violence. Thus the Mayor of Elizabeth, New Jersey, issued an executive order "to shoot to kill" looters, if such action seemed warranted in the individual judgment of the police. If simple order, no matter how much violence it may inflict upon human life, is our basic goal, then those like Mayor Thomas Dunn of Elizabeth are reasonable in resorting to repression in the interests of the public peace.

On the other hand, if the maintenance of such a static conception of order is to be our goal, then there will also come to the fore admittedly amiable and sensitive men like Newark's black Willie Wright, controversial former Vice President of Newark's United Community Corporation. Willie Wright has urged black men—and those who would join them in what he sees as the movement for human liberation—to develop a black "Ace of Spades," a trump card to be held as a counterthreat to any repetition of overt violence and massacre of human life by white people. (The Office of Economic Opportunity threatened to withhold federal funds following the July rebellion in Newark, unless Mr. Wright was removed from Newark's antipoverty board. The board voted its agreement with his basic stand and no funds have been withheld.) Willie Wright says:

Our attack is on a system. Under pressure, our people have destroyed property. It is the others who have devalued human life all along who now resort to the wanton destruction of human life. The alleged snipers in Newark remain "alleged." Many of us have reason to believe that they are white, with the same outlook as that of the white troopers and guardsmen who were seen at night shooting into stores owned by black people with the apparent complicity and encouragement of their superiors.

If some of the snipers were black—and this is not a proven fact—this in itself would be a strange sign of hope that black men will stand up even in a crazy way to defend themselves against wanton massacre.

But such will not be our crazed course for the future, if we are to be killed by men who crave the blood of black men more than they honor decency.

We may or may not agree either with the Thomas Dunns or with the Willie Wrights throughout our land. But the practical choice they represent is clear.

Yet those who advise our leaders in government know, even as our businessmen and industrialists know, that we live in a changing society. They know that it is in the context of a changing society that human values are to be preserved. If businessmen and industrialists were not aware of imminent and continuing changes that lie ahead, they could not prepare for their concerns' survival. In the field of public policy, however, we have not begun to prepare realistically for anticipated change, much of which is already upon us. Although his words may be partisan, Senator Clifford Case of New Jersey issued a clear warning in this regard. "Despite all its passionate words," said Senator Case, "the administration has failed to face up to the dimensions of the problems that beset our cities. The President has spoken often—but his actions belie his words." What the Senator has said of the President may be applied almost universally. The President, after all, is guided for good and for ill by the sentiments of those among and for whom he serves.

It was suggested earlier that there may be illumination for our present civic distress in the basic observations on the social response to frustration made by Robert L. Sutherland more than twenty years ago. Observing repression and aggression in a southern town in relations between black and white people, Sutherland concluded that the institutionalized patterns of behavior were responses to the condition of extended frustration. He noted that the form of reaction to white repression on the part of individual black people was related to the socioeconomic class background of the black person involved. Lower class reaction patterns included malingering and petty acts of aggression. Middle-class responses tended toward withdrawal of patronage from offending merchants. Upper-class responses were expressed more as challenges to institutional structures.

Sutherland's fundamental thesis may be applied to white attitudes of repression. The white counterpart of black lower-class petty aggression would be petty intimidation. White middle-class response would be reflected in the withholding of jobs, loans, or credit. Upper-class repression would express itself in varied forms of paternalism, reinforced by etiquette and law. What we see as happening to our distraught black urban masses is but an enlarged reflection of conditions in the nation at large.

LOCKED AT THE BOTTOM

Hence, the rock-throwing and petty looting under circumstances of open and aggressive rebellion in our cities find their counterpart among lower-class white people in gang fights, threats, and publicly condoned massacre by the police. These people strike out with what they have at hand for things that seem precious. The black and white poor and nearly poor of the cities have been misled concerning circumstances vital to their growth and fulfillment. Among the most devastating signs of our national failure to commit ourselves to the promotion of human dignity and worth are the conditions of the underprivileged white poor and nearly poor in our cities and elsewhere

But people who are spat upon continually sooner or later rebel. Sometimes the rebellion comes in the form of suicide. So it is that those who are white, and are caught in our cities, help lock black people into the dependency for which they must pay the major freight. White people left in our cities have lives, like those of black people, that are marked by aggressive self-hate. "How else could we as white people be left to suffer in the mounting chaos of the city," they must ask, "if we were not too unfortunate to escape?"

While the largest ethnic percentage of students dropping out of schools in our cities are black, the largest absolute numbers are white. Then again, there are more white drop-outs in our metropolitan regions' suburbs than in the black belts of our central cities. The poor and the powerless, black or white, in suburban or city homes, are plundered.

Lee Rainwater has written of the continual sense of exploitation and plunder experienced by the white and black lower classes in our cities. Here are a few samples of what he has to say:

The threatening world of the lower class comes to be absorbed in a world view which generalizes the belief that the environment is threatening more than it is rewarding—that rewards reflect the infrequent working of good luck and that danger is endemic.

Symbolic violence on the part of caretakers (all those whose occupations bring them into contact with lower class people as purveyors of some private or public service) seems also endemic in slum and public housing areas. Students of the interactions between care-takers and their lower class clients have suggested that there is a great deal of punitiveness and shaming commonly expressed by the care-takers in an effort to control and direct the activities of their clients.

The defense of the client is generally one of avoidance, or sullen-ness and feigned stupidity, when contact cannot be avoided. As David Caplovitz has shown so well, lower class people are subjected to con-siderable exploitation by the commercial services with which they deal, and exploitation for money, sexual favors, and sadistic impulses is not unknown on the part of public servants either.

With respect to the exercise of responsibility, we find that parents feel they must bring their children safely through childhood in a world which both poses great physical and moral dangers, and which seeks constantly to seduce them into a way of life which the parent wishes them to avoid. Thus, childrearing becomes an anxious and uncertain process. Two of the most common results are a pervasive repressive-ness in child discipline and training, and, when that seems to fail or is no longer possible, a fatalistic abdication of efforts to protect the children. From the child's point of view, because his parents are not able to protect him from many unpleasantnesses and even from him-self, he loses faith in them and comes to regard them as persons of relatively little consequence.[1]

In such a manner we do violence to those who seem to have no power to control their fortunes; but soon or late we must all learn that those who have nothing to lose do not mind having others share in their bleak condition.

CAUGHT IN THE MIDDLE

The behavior of those who call for the boycotts of stores and schools on the one hand and of those who carry out the job and housing discrimination policies implicit in our institutional life on the other is reflective of deep-rooted civil strife. It is the middle-class people, white and black, who are literally "caught in the middle." Although others make the decisions, they are em-ployed to act.

It is the middle-class district manager in the chain store who must overcharge the poor in the city. Table XVIII shows "Modal

[1] Rainwater, "Fear and the House-As-Haven in the Lower Class," in *AIP Journal*, January 1966, pp. 26, 28, 29.

Prices for Food Items in Higher and Lower Income Areas in Boston, Massachusetts." It reflects a condition of continuous looting of the poor that is carried out by the middle-class agent of big business.

TABLE XVIII   Modal Prices for Food Items in Higher and Lower Income Areas in Boston, Massachusetts

| | LOW INCOME AREA | | HIGHER INCOME | DISCOUNT |
ITEM	CHAINS	INDEPENDENTS	AREA	STORE
Milk				
Half Gallon	50	51	49	49
Gallon	97	99	95	95
Coffee (lb.)				
Reg. (Chock Full-o-Nuts)	89	93, 95	87	87
Butter (Land O Lakes)	85	89	85	85
Margerine (Tri-nut)	36	38	34	34
Flour (5 lbs.)	67	65	63	62
Potatoes (10 lbs.)	69	69	67	65
Sugar (5 lbs.)	61	61	60	58

Meats showed similar tendencies.
Courtesy of Dr. Ivory Lyons, Department of Economics, Northeastern University, Boston, Massachusetts.

Albert Black, Chairman of the Newark Commission for Human Rights, surveyed the stores in the area torn by the July rebellion and noted higher prices in Newark for the identical food items in the same chains of stores in the suburbs. One notorious example of price-hiking was uncovered in Boston several years ago when one chain charged a dollar more for cooking oil in its store patronized by black people than it did for the same item in a store less than two miles away and patronized largely by white people.

White middle-class people managed the chain operations along

Twelfth Street in Detroit that bore the brunt of the fury of black rebellion. White middle-class people operate the housing agencies and employment offices; and yet they wring their hands in innocence when called to task and cry monster when black people strike back in ways at their disposal.

During hearings of the New Jersey Advisory Committee to the United States Commission on Civil Rights, the Hon. Herbert Tate, one of the members of the panel, learned of job openings available through the State Employment Service. He inquired as to whom several potential applicants should report; he was given the specific details, and when the four black girls reported no one knew just what the situation was. The girls called the member of the civil rights panel. "Some mistake must have been made," was the eventual answer given the Commission panelist.

To speak of such behavior as overt and deliberate discrimination is to invite endless debate. Doubtless it is often the unconscious result of cultural perceptions through which we are motivated to see and act accordingly to culturally conditioned ways. What is called for is a national assessment of our values, without which those caught in the middle will be forever vacillating between conflicting opinions as between truth and tradition, conscience and custom. Mr. Tate, however, raises the question of the black community's own immediate responsibility. He asks: "When will we learn that our response to people who have no power is always one such as we would give to children? Until black people collectively represent a power to be dealt with seriously, white people will unconsciously and inevitably treat them as children."

Because he is limited in the fulfillment of his potential by the downward pull of the status of the black community, the middle-class black person, capable and trained, is caught in the middle as well. But again his response to the situation of his middle- and lower-class white and black brothers is potentially the most creative in the nation. The positive and growing militancy of black middle-class teachers is calculated to benefit the teaching craft, as well as those who are taught. Black clergy are seeking a renewal of Christian theology by discovering in empowering answers to the gross needs in our society a modern expression of what they consider the divine plan for man's redemption.

It was the black middle-class whose numbers dominated the July 20–23, 1967, National Conference on Black Power in Newark. They came in response to an agenda set by youthful black militants who were crying out for a reappraisal of values and priorities. The *New York Times* on Saturday, July 22, editorialized on the work of the conference under the caption "Black Phoenix":

> The words "Black power" suggest chauvinism and militancy for some dark purpose. They need not. The National Conference on Black Power now meeting in Newark could do much to bring a constructive meaning to the phrase.
>
> The conference was planned for Newark long before the riots occurred there. Following the disorders, Governor Hughes requested its postponement or transfer because of lingering tensions. But the very existence of these tensions is a strong reason for holding talks in a city where there should have been lingering dialogue to ease the tensions in the first place.
>
> What the Negroes meeting in Newark and elsewhere are saying, primarily among themselves, is: This is largely our problem; sympathy, piety and white concern are not enough; the times now demand more than anger—though anger, too, can be constructive. The conference chairman, Dr. Nathan Wright, Jr., who is Executive Director of the Department of Urban Work in the Episcopal Diocese of Newark, puts it this way: "An assembly of black Americans for serious introspection concerning problems in our own household . . ."
>
> For the first time representatives of almost every Negro group are sitting down together—from the Student Nonviolent Coordinating Committee to the Urban League, from the National Association for the Advancement of Colored People to the Black Muslims. And they are meeting in a combat zone where the results of not digging deeply for causes and solutions are clearly visible.
>
> The governor of New Jersey has named a committee of his own to find the answers to the riots, including whites and Negroes. Senator Brooke of Massachusetts is asking the Senate to appoint a select committee for the same purpose, adding that he does not believe that "outside agitators" cause riots. These governmental studies are all to the good.
>
> But the self-examination that the National Conference on Black Power is now making could be the most enlightening and thought-provoking of all. A new phoenix of hope could rise from the ashes of Newark if something more than a mere echo of the cry "black power" were to be heard.
>
> It is not the term "black power," but what it can signal to the Negro community at large that will mark the real effect of this meet-

ing. Up to now, the most shrill Negro voices have left the impression that "black power" stood for a defeatist form of race separation and violence, as opposed to integration and nonviolence. They have flouted the precepts of the most respected Negro leader in the United States, Dr. Martin Luther King, whose organization, fortunately, is represented at the Newark meeting.

"It's only the whites who consider that black power is used only by Negro radicals," Dr. Wright says. He interprets the term to mean nonviolent economic and political power exercised by and on behalf of the Negro. Surely this is not a radical notion to Negroes and whites who recognize that equality and opportunity—and equality of opportunity—in education, housing and jobs, plus full exercise of the franchise, are basic, absolute rights.

On Monday, July 24, another editorial writer, under prevailing immediate misconceptions about the conference, spoke of "The open black racism that dominated Newark's National Conference on Black Power (which) bitterly disappointed all men of goodwill." The Conference was not racist. Its assumptions were new. In retrospect, news media men and scholars—along with many others —look back with appreciation to the admittedly difficult work of that historic and salutory conference.

It was the most substantial symposium in the nation's history on the issue of empowering the powerless for fulfillment. The scholarly papers from the conference are scheduled to be published as early as possible in 1968. The conference developed a means of communication for "operational harmony" never before achieved in the black community. Further, it served the immediate interests of the nation's safety by providing a platform for the expression of understandable resentments long brewing in the breasts of black men. It was this latter unplanned service that ironically was the focus of attack upon the conference by those who sought to see in black power what was and is not there: a mirror image of the abuse of white power. Some papers and other news media have extended their regrets for all-too-hasty and distorted judgments of the National Conference on Black Power, for those who are interested in furthering black power are almost wholly constructive. Their purpose is not basically to please but to help us save ourselves from charted self-destruction.

THE KEEPERS OF THE GATE

Those who stand guard at the gates of the cities' future—and in whose hands lies much of the well-being of the nation—are the upper-class men and women who give basic shape to the institutions of our society. It is they who must see that the possibility of violence is always certain. The honest choices are between the kinds of potential violence that confront us. Violence to the human spirit is rampant in our cities—and in the households and public life of our suburban communities and elsewhere. Each time one human life fails to find its due fulfillment, the nation's life is lessened; we as a people become less than what we should be.

Violence has long been an uncherished part of our heritage. As Detroit's Otis Saunders reminds us: "Let us not forget the concentration camps which we speak of as Indian Reservations and Relocation Camps (for Japanese Americans in World War II). Lest we forget, these are a part of our uncherished heritage. Then, too, the extermination of the Indian nations was almost as devastating as that of the buffalo. Hitlerian Germany bears some slight resemblance to a heritage which we far too easily forget."

Even the scanning of Otis Saunders' words is painful. Yet we must recognize the depth of the violence that is a part of our lives. Forewarned is—or should be—forearmed.

Violence to those in our central cities is matched by our glossing over of problems in our homes and in our communities; that is, those problems we do not export to the city. Violence is with us. But there is a form of violence, the final purpose of which is hope, peace, and fulfillment. It is the violence to our established attitudes that inevitably comes from change. This violence we must accept for the good it contains. We must rebuild our institutions with flexibility sufficient to adapt to changing conditions. Rigid structures cannot withstand the earthquakes which are—and will be increasingly—a part of our changing times. The alternative is cities in ruin.

Plato, in the *Republic* (Book VII), tells a story that might be a parable for our time. It is worthy of consideration by all in our nation who share in the keeping of the cities' gates. It is the celebrated parable of the cave.

"Next, then," I said, "take the following parable of education and ignorance as a picture of the condition of our nature. Imagine mankind as dwelling in an underground cave with a long entrance open to the light across the whole width of the cave; in this they have been from childhood, with necks and legs fettered, so they have to stay where they are. They cannot move their heads round because of the fetters, and they can only look forward, but light comes to them from fire burning behind them higher up at a distance. Between the fire and the prisoners is a road above their level, and along it imagine a low wall has been built, as puppet showmen have screens in front of their people over which they work their puppets."

"I see," he said.

"See, then, bearers carrying along this wall all sorts of articles which they hold projecting above the wall, statues of men and other living things, made of stone or wood and all kinds of stuff, some of the bearers speaking and some silent, as you might expect."

"What a remarkable image," he said, "and what remarkable prisoners!"

"Just like ourselves," I said. "For, first of all, tell me this: What do you think such people would have seen of themselves and each other except their shadows, which the fire cast on the opposite wall of the cave?"

"I don't see how they could see anything else," said he, "if they were compelled to keep their heads unmoving all their lives!"

"Very well, what of the things being carried along? Would not this be the same?"

"Of course it would."

"Suppose the prisoners were able to talk together, don't you think that when they named the shadows which they saw passing they would believe they were naming things?"

"Necessarily."

"Then if their prison had an echo from the opposite wall, whenever one of the passing bearers uttered a sound, would they not suppose that the passing shadow must be making the sound? Don't you think so?"

"Indeed I do," he said.

"If so," said I, "such persons would certainly believe that there were no realities except those shadows of handmade things."

"So it must be," said he.

"Now consider," said I, "what their release would be like, and their cure from these fetters and their folly; let us imagine whether it might naturally be something like this. One might be released, and compelled suddenly to stand up and turn his neck round, and to walk and look towards the firelight; all this would hurt him, and he would be too much dazzled to see distinctly those things whose shadows he had seen before. What do you think he would say, if someone told him that what he saw before was foolery, but now he saw more rightly, being a bit nearer reality and turned towards what was a little more real? What if he were shown each of the passing things, and compelled by questions to answer what each one was? Don't you think he would be puzzled, and believe what he saw before was more true than what was shown to him now?"

"And if he should have to compete with those who had been always prisoners, by laying down the law about those shadows while he was blinking before his eyes were settled down—and it would take a good long time to get used to things—wouldn't they all laugh at him and say he had spoiled his eyesight by going up there, and it was not worthwhile so much as to try to go up? And would they not kill anyone who tried to release them and take them up, if they could somehow lay hands on him and kill him?"

"That they would!" said he.

Our present condition resembles the predicament of those confined in Plato's cave. Not one among us knows precisely what lies ahead. But the restless and distraught in our cities, who are most keenly aware that life must become far more than it is or has been, may at this hour be calling us toward a greater perception of the realities that promise fulfillment.

Even the orderly change of which we speak will not be easy; change is always dislocating. Yet distress and dislocation of various kinds are already upon us. Unplanned change is in conflict with a static conception of order that comes through to growing numbers as effective repression. Our current conception of order lacks the flexibility sufficient for orderly change. While we may not end the conflict, we may shift the scene of the battle to include more constructive choices.

The alternatives we have as a nation are brought into focus by our cities, which have been marked most clearly by a condition of continuous riot. While there is time, we may still choose between life and death. We may seek to grow with the times and survive; or we may continue to hold stubbornly to the past and perish.